First World War
and Army of Occupation
War Diary
France, Belgium and Germany

3 DIVISION
7 Infantry Brigade
Honourable Artillery Company
1 Battalion Honourable Artillery Company
12 September 1914 - 16 June 1915

WO95/1415/4

The Naval & Military Press Ltd
www.nmarchive.com
Published in association with The National Archives

Published by

The Naval & Military Press Ltd

Unit 10 Ridgewood Industrial Park,

Uckfield, East Sussex,

TN22 5QE England

Tel: +44 (0) 1825 749494

www.naval-military-press.com

www.nmarchive.com

This diary has been reprinted in facsimile from the original. Any imperfections are inevitably reproduced and the quality may fall short of modern type and cartographic standards.

© **Crown Copyright**
Images reproduced by permission of The National Archives, London, England, 2015.

Contents

Document type	Place/Title	Date From	Date To
Heading	WO95/1415 3 Div 7 Infantry Bde Hon Artillery Coy Aug 1914-June 1915		
Heading	3rd Division 7th Infy Bde Honourable Artillery Company 1914 Sep-1915 June Beeam G H Q Troops		
Heading	7th Infantry Bde. 3rd Division. Honourable Artillery Company September, 1914 (Diary commences 12.9.1914)		
War Diary	Headquarters Armoury House, London	12/09/1914	12/09/1914
War Diary	Belhus Park Essex	13/09/1914	15/09/1914
War Diary	Belhus Park	15/09/1914	18/09/1914
War Diary	At Sea	19/09/1914	20/09/1914
War Diary	St Nazaire	21/09/1914	23/09/1914
War Diary	Le Mans	24/09/1914	03/10/1914
Heading	7th Infantry Brigade. 3rd Division Honourable Artillery Company October 1914 (went to 8th Bde 9 Novr)		
War Diary	Le Mans	01/10/1914	31/10/1914
Heading	8th Infantry Brigade 3rd Division. Honourable Artillery Company November 1914 (Joined Brigade 9.11.1914 from 7th Infy. Bde.)		
War Diary	Travelling & arrival at St Omer	01/11/1914	01/11/1914
War Diary	St Omer	02/11/1914	04/11/1914
War Diary	St Omer to Bailleul	05/11/1914	05/11/1914
War Diary	Bailleul	06/11/1914	07/11/1914
War Diary	Estaires	08/11/1914	08/11/1914
War Diary	Les Lobes	09/11/1914	16/11/1914
War Diary	Les Lobes to Bailleul	16/11/1914	17/11/1914
War Diary	Bailleul	18/11/1914	20/11/1914
War Diary	Bailleul to Neuve Eglise	21/11/1914	21/11/1914
War Diary	Neuve Eglise	22/11/1914	27/11/1914
War Diary	Neuve Eglise to Westoutre	27/11/1914	29/11/1914
War Diary	Westoutre to Sherpenberg	30/11/1914	01/12/1914
Heading	7th Infantry Bde. 3rd Division. Honourable Artillery Company December 1914 (Joined 7th Bde. 8.12.14 from 8th Bde.)		
War Diary	Sherpenberg	01/12/1914	03/12/1914
War Diary	Sherpenberg to Kemmel	03/12/1914	03/12/1914
War Diary	Kemmel	04/12/1914	06/12/1914
War Diary	Kemmel to Westoutre	06/12/1914	06/12/1914
War Diary	Westoutre	07/12/1914	08/12/1914
War Diary	Westoutre to Kemmel	09/12/1914	09/12/1914
War Diary	Kemmel	09/12/1914	12/12/1914
War Diary	Locre	13/12/1914	15/12/1914
War Diary	Locre to Kemmel	15/12/1914	15/12/1914
War Diary	Kemmel	16/12/1914	18/12/1914
War Diary	Kemmel to Locre	18/12/1914	18/12/1914
War Diary	Locre	19/12/1914	24/12/1914
War Diary	Locre to Kemmel	24/12/1914	24/12/1914
War Diary	Kemmel	25/12/1914	27/12/1914
War Diary	Kemmel to Westoutre	27/12/1914	27/12/1914
War Diary	Westoutre	28/12/1914	31/12/1914

Heading	7th Inf. Bde. 3rd Div. War Diary 1st Battn. The Honourable Artillery Company. January 1915		
War Diary	Locre	01/01/1915	04/01/1915
War Diary	Kemmel	05/01/1915	08/01/1915
War Diary	Locre	09/01/1915	12/01/1915
War Diary	Kemmel	13/01/1915	16/01/1915
War Diary	Locre	17/01/1915	20/01/1915
War Diary	Kemmel	21/01/1915	24/01/1915
War Diary	Locre	25/01/1915	28/01/1915
War Diary	Kemmel	29/01/1915	31/01/1915
Heading	7th Inf. Bde. 3rd Div. War Diary 1st Battn. The Honourable Artillery Company. February 1915		
War Diary		01/02/1915	28/02/1915
Heading	7th Inf. Bde. 3rd Div. War Diary 1st Battn. The Honourable Artillery Company. March 1915		
War Diary	Locre	01/03/1915	04/03/1915
War Diary	Kemmel	05/03/1915	16/03/1915
War Diary	Kemmel to Westoutre	17/03/1915	17/03/1915
War Diary	Westoutre	18/03/1915	23/03/1915
War Diary	Westoutre to St Eloi	23/03/1915	23/03/1915
War Diary	St Eloi	24/03/1915	27/03/1915
War Diary	Dickebusch	28/03/1915	29/03/1915
War Diary	St Eloi	30/03/1915	31/03/1915
Heading	7th Inf. Bde. 3rd Div. War Diary 1st Battn. The Honourable Artillery Company. April 1915		
War Diary	Dickebusch	01/04/1915	04/04/1915
War Diary	St Eloi	05/04/1915	08/04/1915
War Diary	Dickebusch	09/04/1915	12/04/1915
War Diary	St Eloi	13/04/1915	16/04/1915
War Diary	Dickebusch	17/04/1915	20/04/1915
War Diary	St Eloi	21/04/1915	24/04/1915
War Diary	Dickebusch	25/04/1915	28/04/1915
War Diary	St Eloi	29/04/1915	30/04/1915
Heading	7th Inf. Bde. 3rd Div. War Diary 1st Battn. The Honourable Artillery Company. May 1915		
War Diary	St Eloi	01/05/1915	02/05/1915
War Diary	Dickebusch	03/05/1915	06/05/1915
War Diary	Ridgewood	07/05/1915	11/05/1915
War Diary	Elzenwalle	12/05/1915	17/05/1915
War Diary	Ridgewood	18/05/1915	21/05/1915
War Diary	Elzenwalle	22/05/1915	25/05/1915
War Diary	Ridgewood	26/05/1915	29/05/1915
War Diary	Elzenwalle	30/05/1915	31/05/1915
Heading	7th Inf. Bde. 3rd Div. War Diary 1st Battn. The Honourable Artillery Company. June (1.6.15 to 16.6.15) 1915		
War Diary	Elzenwalle	01/06/1915	02/06/1915
War Diary	Vlamertinge	03/06/1915	05/06/1915
War Diary	Ypres	05/06/1915	08/06/1915
War Diary	Hooge	09/06/1915	16/06/1915

WO 95/1415

3 DIV 7 INFANTRY BDE

Army 1914-1918

Don. Artillery Coy

Aug 1914 - Jun 1915

3RD DIVISION
7TH INFY BDE

HONOURABLE ARTILLERY COMPANY
~~SEPT — DECR 1914.~~

1914 SEP — 1915 JUNE

Became GHQ Troops.

7th Infantry Bde.
3rd Division.

HONOURABLE ARTILLERY COMPANY

SEPTEMBER, 1 9 1 4

(Diary commences 12.9.1914)

Army Form C. 2118.

WAR DIARY
or
INTELLIGENCE SUMMARY.

(Erase heading not required.)

I   N.A. Coy.

Instructions regarding War Diaries and Intelligence Summaries are contained in F. S. Regs., Part II. and the Staff Manual respectively. Title pages will be prepared in manuscript.

Hour, Date, Place	Summary of Events and Information	Remarks and references to Appendices
1914		
12th SEPTEMBER 9.30 a.m.	Service Battalion paraded. The CAPTAIN-GENERAL His	H.A.C.
11 a.m.	Majesty the KING arrived & inspected the Battalion. He remarked that the Battalion looked finer recruits	
HEADQUARTERS	them every success & a safe return. Finally all the	G.S.
ARMOURY HOUSE, LONDON	officers were presented to the CAPTAIN-GENERAL.	
	The Battalion marched to ST PANCRAS STATION & entrained for PURFLEET RIFLE RANGE STATION where they detrained and marched to camp at BELHUS PARK	
13d BELHUS PARK ESSEX	Busy cleaning & getting Camp in order	G.S.
14th "	No 3 Coy. RAINHAM RIFLE RANGES. Remainder field Exercises & route marches. No 1 Coy outpost duty at night.	G.S.
15th "	No 1 Coy. Route march. No 4 RAINHAM RIFLE RANGES - No 2 & 3 Coys Field Exercises. No 2 Outpost duty at night	G.S.

WAR DIARY or INTELLIGENCE SUMMARY.

Army Form C. 2118.

Hour, Date, Place	Summary of Events and Information	Remarks and references to Appendices
SEPTEMBER 1914		
15th contd. BELHUS PARK	C.O. lectured Officers & NCO's on Entrenching. C.O. received following telephone message from WAR OFFICE "Your T.	
2.30pm	Battalion is to be held in readiness to embark at an early date. It will proceed at the War Establishment laid down for an infantry battalion on pages 142-146 war Establishment part 7 1914. All personnel proceeding with the battalion must be medically fit for service, fully trained and nineteen years of age and any personnel surplus to establishment should be turned over to reserve battalion. Telegraph whether full establishment of personnel fulfilling these conditions is available."	F2 H.A.C.
6.9pm	Telegram received from United London (London District) as above.	no. F2 H.A.C.
6.34pm	Reply "Infantry Battalion H.A.C. requires 6 ASC drivers & 5 RAMC orderlies to complete War Establishment. The former can be filled from Reserve Battalion etc.	F3

WAR DIARY
or
INTELLIGENCE SUMMARY.
(Erase heading not required.)

Army Form C. 2118.

Hour, Date, Place		Summary of Events and Information	Remarks and references to Appendices
SEPTEMBER - 1914			
15th Contd BELHUS PARK		"500 men are recruits & not fully trained although most of them have had previous training in O.T.C. From O.C. H.A.C. TO O.C.TED LONDON.	VI.
16d "	9am	Parade for C.O. No1 Company RAINHAM RIFLE RANGE. Telegrams received with regard to Establishment to proceed overseas, Inspection of Transport by Sa Dremount, Train accommodation, Field Dressings, Rifle equipment.	V.
17d "		Hard work all day getting ready. Officers sword	
	5pm	sharpened. Boots & equipment arrived here	V.
		served out. Telegrams received re Transport, Part II	
	10 pm	Orders. Rifles & Bayonets arrived & were served out	
18t "	1 am	Finished serving out rifles & bayonets.	VI.
	2:45am	Parade Right Half Battalion & Headquarters	

WAR DIARY
or
INTELLIGENCE SUMMARY.
(Erase heading not required.)

Army Form C. 2118.

Hour, Date, Place	Summary of Events and Information	Remarks and references to Appendices
SEPTEMBER 1914		
18th contd BELHUS PARK 4:35am	Entrained after marching to PURFLEET OLD STATION	
6.30am	left station: arrived SOUTHAMPTON 12½ am.	
6:28am	Left H.Q/Battalion arrived PURFLEET OLD STATION ?	
	Entrained left at 8.30 am arrived SOUTHAMPTON 1.45 pm	
	Embarked on board S.S. "WESTMEATH". No hitch	S1
4.35 pm	left SOUTHAMPTON. Telegram received re Waterbottles.	
19th " AT SEA	On board S.S. WESTMEATH.	S1
20d "	On board S.S. WESTMEATH	S1
10 am	arrived off ST NAZAIRE. Disembarkation commenced	
	at 6.30 p.m. No 4 Coy continued unloading all	
	night. Marched to CASINO & REST CAMP – some of	
	the Battalion being quartered at each place.	
21st ST NAZAIRE	C.O. Parade 10 am.	S3

WAR DIARY or INTELLIGENCE SUMMARY.

Army Form C. 2118.

Hour, Date, Place	Summary of Events and Information	Remarks and references to Appendices
SEPTEMBER 1914		
22nd ST NAZAIRE	Warning received on telephone one company would go to NANTES, 2 Companies to LE MANS & 1 would remain at ST NAZAIRE.	
3 p.m.	Capt WARD & No 3 Coy left for NANTES	See appendix No 1 for No 3 Coy during their stay at NANTES
23rd "	No 1 & 2 Companies Headquarters marched to ST NAZAIRE Station & entrained at 1 p.m. & left at 1.35 p.m. for LE MANS via NANTES & ANGERS. No 4 Coy with Major HANSON (2nd in command) & CAPT COLE remained behind.	SA See appendix No 2 for No 4 Coy during they stay at ST NAZAIRE
		EA
24th LE MANS 12.30 a.m.	arrived at LE MANS STATION & main body marched to camp. Baggage etc arrived 6.30 a.m. in camp.	
10 a.m.	Colonel A. GRAHAM THOMPSON C.B. (Commandant advanced Base) visited camp. Orderlies detailed for Mq & A.B.O. in France	EA
3 p.m.	Capt GARNSEY left with 1 Platoons of No 2 Coy for HAVRE.	See appendix No 3 for ½ Company No 2 at HAVRE

WAR DIARY or INTELLIGENCE SUMMARY.

Army Form C. 2118.

Hour, Date, Place		Summary of Events and Information	Remarks and references to Appendices
SEPTEMBER 1914			
25th LE MANS		Battalion changed quarters. Inspected by Commandant A.B.D. Col ABRAHAM THOMPSON C.B. Marched to AVENUE PONT LIEUE. Some quartered in the Period Schools in RUE DE REPOS + remainder in L'ECOLE VÉRON DE FORT BONNAIS. 4Cpl SMART. C. Transport Section taken to HOSPITAL. Found orderlies for SIGNAL OFFICE etc.	
26th "		3 Officers & 120 men warned to be in readiness to proceed to HAVRE. Corpl MALLINSON & 2 men proceeded to BANQUE DE FRANCE + went as Coach escort to GHQ at the FRONT	
27th "	9am	Church Parade. Inoculation commenced. Orders received cancelling warning for 3 Officers & 120 men for HAVRE. Church	
	6pm	Parade Jacobus Theatre.	
28th "		No 1 Coy exercise in Trench Digging. No 2 Coy Route March.	

WAR DIARY
or
INTELLIGENCE SUMMARY.
(Erase heading not required.)

Army Form C. 2118.

Hour, Date, Place	Summary of Events and Information	Remarks and references to Appendices
SEPTEMBER 1914		
29th LE MANS	Visit from COMMANDANT. No 1 Coy engaged in Bridging stream.	S1
30th "	No 2 Coy exercised in Trench Digging. Corporal MALLINSON (with 2 men) returned from Cook escort duty. Orders received to hold 1 Company in readiness to proceed to HAVRE.	S1
OCTOBER 1914		
1st LE MANS	No Exercise in Trench Digging. Orders received that 2 Platoons only to be in readiness to proceed to HAVRE.	S1
2nd "	C.O visited all Guard Posts (Railway, MAROC etc). Capt WHYTE left with remainder of No 2 Coy (2 platoons) for HAVRE	S1
3rd "	M.O. (Lt CARNWATH) left for NANTES with an orderly to inoculate No 3 Company. Inoculation continued here under Lt DOBSON	S1

7th Infantry Brigade.
3rd Division

HONOURABLE ARTILLERY COMPANY

OCTOBER 1914

(went to 8" Bde 9 Nov)

Army Form C. 2118.

WAR DIARY
OF
INTELLIGENCE SUMMARY.
(Erase heading not required.)

Instructions regarding War Diaries and Intelligence Summaries are contained in F. S. Regs., Part II. and the Staff Manual respectively. Title pages will be prepared in manuscript.

Place	Date	Hour	Summary of Events and Information	Remarks and references to Appendices
LE MANS	1914 Oct. 1		No. 2 Exercise in Trench Digging. Orders received that two platoons only to be in readiness to proceed to Havre.	
	2		C.O. visited all Guard Posts (Railway, MAROC, etc.) Capt. WHYTE left with remainder of No. 2 Coy. (2 platoons) for HAVRE.	
	3		M.O. (Lt. CARNWATH) left for NANTES with an orderly to inoculate No. 3 Company. Inoculation continued here under Lt. Dobson.	

Army Form C. 2118.

WAR DIARY
or
INTELLIGENCE SUMMARY.
(Erase heading not required.)

Instructions regarding War Diaries and Intelligence Summaries are contained in F. S. Regs., Part II. and the Staff Manual respectively. Title pages will be prepared in manuscript.

Hour, Date, Place			Summary of Events and Information	Remarks and references to Appendices
OCTOBER	1914			
4th	LE MANS	9.30am	Church Parade. COMMANDANT inspected Billets.	S1
5th	"		Officers Staff Ride :- output positions & sketching at CHANGÉ	S1
6th	"		Officers Staff Ride :- similar work to 5th at RUADIN	S1
7th	"		Bayonet Exercises, Fire Discipline mental for all not on guards, under ADJUTANT.	S1
8th	"		Bayonet Exercises. Inoculations still continuing. Pte HURD sent to hospital.	S1
9th	"		M.O. (Lt. CARNWATH) returned from NANTES. Officers Staff ride to SPAY.	S1
10th	"		N.C.O's & Junior Officers Fire Discipline mental under ADJUTANT	S1

WAR DIARY
or
INTELLIGENCE SUMMARY.

(Erase heading not required.)

Army Form C. 2118.

Hour, Date, Place	Summary of Events and Information	Remarks and references to Appendices
OCTOBER 1914		
11th LE MANS 8.45am	Communion Service 9.30am. Church Parade. COMMANDANT attended.	OS
12th "	Staff Ride for Officers. Outpost duty between CHANGE & RUAUDIN	OS
13th "	Officers Staff ride 9/12th Continued. Pte GOODALL discharged from Hospital. Pte LANGMAID & HEATH sent to HOSPITAL. 3 NCO's + 60 men to MAROC for fatigue until further orders.	OS
14th "	Pte HEAL discharged from HOSPITAL.	OS
15th "	Officers Staff Ride. Finding defensive position for a Battalion between ST GEORGES DU BOIS & PRUILLÉ, W of LE MANS. Escort of 1 NCO + 3 men sent to HOSPITAL for GERMAN Prisoners A.G. to ST NAZAIRE.	OS
16th "	Officers Staff Ride - yesterdays work Continued. Blankets &,	OS

Army Form C. 2118.

WAR DIARY
or
INTELLIGENCE SUMMARY.

(Erase heading not required.)

10.

Instructions regarding War Diaries and Intelligence Summaries are contained in F. S. Regs., Part II. and the Staff Manual respectively. Title pages will be prepared in manuscript.

Hour, Date, Place	Summary of Events and Information	Remarks and references to Appendices
OCTOBER 1914		
16th Contd LEMANS.	Equipment drawn from depot at MAROC. Major T.C. COOPER President F.G.C.M.	
17th	C.O. visited A.B. Office that interned with COMMANDANT.	S1
"	Pte HURD discharged from HOSPITAL. Clothing drawn from MAROC.	S1
18th	9am Communion Service 9.30am Church Parade.	
"	2.30pm C.O. called for COMMANDANT at A.B. Office motored to ST GEORGES DU BOIS. Met our officers there & COMMANDANT inspected defensive positions taken up on 15.9.16. The site for trenches. He expressed himself pleased with the work done & gave some sound advice.	S1
19th	Officers Staff Ride in neighbourhood of J EYVRÉ. Orders received for escort of 1 NCO + 3 men to call at HOSPITAL for GERMAN Prisoners to go to ST NAZAIRE	S1

Army Form C. 2118.

WAR DIARY
or
INTELLIGENCE SUMMARY.
(Erase heading not required.)

Hour, Date, Place	Summary of Events and Information	Remarks and references to Appendices
OCTOBER 1914		
20th LE MANS	Major COOPER & Officers No 1 Company rode to ARNAGE to work out billeting scheme & out post duty. Pte HEATH discharged from HOSPITAL.	9]
21st "	Officers Staff Ride - Attack & defence scheme E GLEMANS	9]
22nd "	Major COOPER President F.G.C.M - Capt NESHAM a member.	S]
23rd "	Officers Staff Ride - attack on CHANGE - the defensive positions being previously marked on the map by C.O. Major COOPER & Capt NESHAM F.G.C.M as yesterday. Pte STAFFORD sent to Hospital	S]
24th "	Officers Staff Ride in neighbourhood of ARNAGE. Lieut DOBSON member F.G.C.M. Following telegram received:- From Communications to O.C. HAC. LEMANS :- LONDON SCOTTISH	C]

WAR DIARY or INTELLIGENCE SUMMARY.

Army Form C. 2118.

Hour, Date, Place	Summary of Events and Information	Remarks and references to Appendices
OCTOBER 1914		
24th Cont'd LE MANS	are being sent to the front and you will relieve them aaa Fifth Border Regt from Home will relieve you aaa Have ordered Commandant NANTES & ST NAZAIRE to each hold a company of your regiment in readiness to proceed to railhead for duty." Telegram received from Major HANSON saying No4 at ST NAZAIRE had received wire to hold itself in readiness to proceed to railhead & relieve LONDON SCOTTISH	E1
25th 10pm	57 men & Sgt PALMER left for PARIS for Police duty	
" 9am	Communion Service. 9.30 am Church Parade.	E1
"	ADJUTANT availed Headquarters A.B.O. for interview with COMMANDANT	
26d	Received telegram from O.C. No 3 Coy NANTES "Ordered to proceed to ABBEVILLE." They arrived LE MANS Station 5.30pm & left for ABBEVILLE 6.45 p.m. Received telegram from Major HANSON "No4 Coy to proceed to ABBEVILLE, All well".	E1

WAR DIARY
or
INTELLIGENCE SUMMARY.

(Erase heading not required.)

Army Form C. 2118.

Instructions regarding War Diaries and Intelligence Summaries are contained in F. S. Regs., Part II. and the Staff Manual respectively. Title pages will be prepared in manuscript.

Hour, Date, Place		Summary of Events and Information	Remarks and references to Appendices
OCTOBER 1914			
27. LE MANS	5.30am	Cpl SMART died in hospital. C.O wired his parents. Capt COLE & No1 Company have passed through here 11.15am. Major HANSON reported ill & was left at ST NAZAIRE. Major COOPER left in afternoon with 2 platoons of No 1 Company for ABBEVILLE.	ST
28	9.30am	C.O representative of the regiment attended funeral of CPL SMART at military Cemetary - Transport Section found the bearer party. Heard from I.G.C. that the Battalion would proceed to the front as soon as relieved. 2h COMMANDANT waited on us and arranged for us to draw G S Wagons, S. A. Carts & Water Cart. (Heavy rain first really wet day). Wires received from Major COOPER saying "all safe at ABBEVILLE" from Capt WARD reporting safe arrival of No 3 rt Companies at ST OMER (G.HQ). Detachment under Capt B. SMITH 5th BORDER REGT (T) arrived 6 pm.	ST
29			ST

WAR DIARY or INTELLIGENCE SUMMARY.

Army Form C. 2118.

14

(Erase heading not required.)

Hour, Date, Place	Summary of Events and Information	Remarks and references to Appendices
OCTOBER 1914		
29th (Contd) LE MANS	to relieve us – they were quartered in Communal Schools. Orders received to draw more S.A.A. Carts, wagons & horses also hand we shall probably leave tomorrow.	
30th "	Orders received to move to ABBEVILLE at 3 p.m. These orders were cancelled when the transport had arrived at the station. Orders received for transport to entrain & that the Batn would move tomorrow.	
31st "	Headquarters remaining 2 Platoons of No 1 Coy & Transport left LE MANS 7.45am via ROUEN for ABBEVILLE.	

NOTE:- JOINED 8th INFY BDE. 9th NOVR. 1914

8th Infantry Brigade
3rd Division.

HONOURABLE ARTILLERY COMPANY

NOVEMBER 1 9 1 4

(Joined Brigade 9.11.1914)
from 7th Infy.Bde.

Army Form C. 2118.

1st — H.A.C.
JOINED B.E.F 9 Nov 1914

WAR DIARY
or
INTELLIGENCE SUMMARY.
(Erase heading not required.)

Instructions regarding War Diaries and Intelligence Summaries are contained in F. S. Regs., Part II. and the Staff Manual respectively. Title pages will be prepared in manuscript.

Hour, Date, Place	Summary of Events and Information	Remarks and references to Appendices
NOVEMBER 1914		
1. Travelling & arrival at ST OMER	Arrived ABBEVILLE 11am. Picked up Major COOPER & 2 Platoons of No 1 Coy – Ordered to go on to ST OMER – Proceeded via BOULOGNE & CALAIS Reached ST OMER 8pm. met at Station by Capt WHYTE. (Heard LONDON SCOTTISH had been in action & sustained considerable losses) Quartered in SOLFERINO BARRACKS. Found No 2 Coy already at ST OMER – This was the first intimation that they had received orders to leave HAVRE. Capt GARNSEY with remainder of No 2 Coy arrived late at night from ROUEN.	E1
2. ST OMER	(Found Capt LINDSEY & 50 men of LONDON SCOTTISH also at these barracks. News that they had severe casualties but behaved splendidly) No 3rd Companies marched out and were trained in trench digging all day. C.O had a talk with General CHICHESTER the Brigade Major and suggested we should not be sent	E1

(9 29 6) W 2791 100,000 8/14 H W V   Forms/C. 2118/11.

WAR DIARY
or
INTELLIGENCE SUMMARY.
(Erase heading not required.)

Army Form C. 2118.

Hour, Date, Place	Summary of Events and Information	Remarks and references to Appendices
NOVEMBER 1914 ST. OMER 2nd Contd	into action unless absolutely necessary & asked first to go with the Brigade Reserve so that men might become accustomed to shell fire. also noted we had never fired our rifles. (He seemed rather astonished but reiterated promised every assurance).	[1]
3rd "	The Battalion went trench digging to the same place as yesterday. The C.O. met General LAMBTON (Military Secretary to the C in C) & said he hoped H.A.C. would be given a fair chance & not thrown into action too soon & suggested they should first go in reserve in order to become accustomed to shell rifle fire &c by this means better results would be obtained. He also said we had 600 recruits & the men had never had a chance of sighting their rifles.	[2]
4th "	The C.O.'s conversations with authorities evidently	[3]

WAR DIARY or INTELLIGENCE SUMMARY.

Army Form C. 2118.

Hour, Date, Place	Summary of Events and Information	Remarks and references to Appendices
NOVEMBER 1914		
4th ST OMER	took effect) Rifle Range in town ditch allotted to us all day. No 1 Coy. Signallers & Pioneers all had 5 shots each at Silhouette targets. Found rifles mostly sighted 50 yards low. Light bad but shooting excellent. Informed by Brigade Major that remaining Companies could fire on following days but this excellent scheme was not fulfilled as orders came in the evening for the whole Battalion to proceed to BAILLEUL by motor bus tomorrow morning.	
5th ST OMER to BAILLEUL	Left ST OMER in motor busses at 9 am. Arrived at BAILLEUL mid-day. Reported to General MORELAN men billeted in peloton. Transport came by road & bivouacked at HAZEBROUCK.	
6th BAILLEUL	Transport arrived 1 pm. Nos 2 & 3 Companies went for a route march across BELGIAN	

WAR DIARY or INTELLIGENCE SUMMARY.

Army Form C. 2118.

Hour, Date, Place	Summary of Events and Information	Remarks and references to Appendices
NOVEMBER 1914 6th Contd BAILLEUL	Frontier. Heard heavy firing but to foggy to see anything of the battle in progress. C. Ocalled on Col MALCOLM of the LONDON SCOTTISH when obtaining account of their affairs that their casualties were something over 300.	
7th "	Nos 1 & 4 Coys went for route march in the direction of MESSINES where they saw many shells bursting etc. Received orders to go by route march to ESTAIRES the same afternoon. Report to LAHORE Division INDIAN CORPS. Left at 4.30 p.m. Mr DOBSON was detailed as guide. The C.O. Considers he did a difficult task. Considering the darkness & strange country, his performance was really admirable. Men billeted on arrival at 8.30 p.m. in a girls school & an old granary.	

WAR DIARY
or
INTELLIGENCE SUMMARY. 19.
(Erase heading not required.)

Army Form C. 2118.

Hour, Date, Place	Summary of Events and Information	Remarks and references to Appendices
NOVEMBER 1914		
8th ESTAIRES	Quiet day. C.O. motored to LAVENTIE with Major BETTINE into//near INDIAN CORPS. Found news utterly destroyed also then went behind the trenches – visited 3 Brigade HQ)	31
9th " 4th LES LOBES	Orders received to proceed by route march to LES LOBES & to report to Brigade Major 8th Infantry Brigade. Left at 12.45pm & arrived LES LOBES 3pm – men billeted in farms near the Brigade Hqrs. General FRENCH the C in C met us on the road & inspected the Battalion. He told the C.O. how pleased he was to have us out & wished us all "good luck" He seemed greatly impressed with the stature of the regiment.	31
10th LES LOBES	General SIR JAMES WILLCOCKS Commanding the INDIAN CORPS inspected the Battalion said he was proud to have such a splendid body of men under his command & hoped we should uphold our great	31

WAR DIARY
or
INTELLIGENCE SUMMARY.

Army Form C. 2118.

20

Hour, Date, Place	Summary of Events and Information	Remarks and references to Appendices
NOVEMBER 1914 10th LES LOBES.	tradition. He also paid General FRENCH invited us to go into the trenches first by companies attached to the regulars in order to become gradually educated to the kind of warfare & afterwards be moved into us as a separate unit. The C.O. inspected some trenches dug by the French Engineers and Col. HOLMAN (Indian Corps). Major COOPER & 200 men went French digging close behind the firing line at ROUGE CROIX. Orders received to act as supports during night operations to be at ZELOBES at 8pm Order of march – Brigade HQrs, ROYAL SCOTS, MIDDLESEX REGT, HAC, marched to CROIX BERBEE (about 5 miles) just behind our lines in front of NEUVE CHAPELLE. The whole Battalion went into support Trenches. At 12/2 midnight, our guns, including several heavy batteries opened a terrific bombardment	81

WAR DIARY
or
INTELLIGENCE SUMMARY.
(Erase heading not required.)

Army Form C. 2118.

2/

Hour, Date, Place	Summary of Events and Information	Remarks and references to Appendices
NOVEMBER 1914		
10th Contd LES LOBES	on NEUVE CHAPELLE – the shells passing over our heads. This lasted until 12"45 am. The Germans did not reply with gun fire but only with severe rifle fire.] We left the Trenches at 3:30 am. returned to our billets arriving there at 6 am.	21
11th	Quiet day in Billets	21
12th	Nov 2,3rd Corps went with C.O. to ROUGE CROIX for trench digging under Major BOILEAU R.E. Men worked well were badly sniped. A No1 Coy under Major COOPER went to CROIX BERBÉE for the same work.	21
13th	Nov 2,3rd Corps went for the same work to ROUGE CROIX and Major BOILEAU R.E. They came under heavy shrapnel & shell fire also rifle fire. The left hand trenches were swept	21

WAR DIARY
INTELLIGENCE SUMMARY.

Army Form C. 2118.

22

Hour, Date, Place	Summary of Events and Information	Remarks and references to Appendices
NOVEMBER 1914.		
13th contd LES LOBES	by latter which made it impossible to dig for at least an hour. Not much work was done as the men had to continually take shelter from shell fire. Rumpers. [The C.O. remarked it was wonderful that we had no casualties.] Major COOPER & No1 Coy went trench digging at CROIX BARBÉE.	81
14th "	No 3 & 4 Corps went to ROUGECROIX for continuation of yesterdays work [under Capt WARD. Major COOPER] No7 & No2 Corps to LA COUTURE for same work. [Adjutant & C.O. remained at HQ as 1 Platoon of each Company was left behind to fulfil orders to go into trenches with the Regulars during the night. These orders were cancelled during the day. At 4pm a cyclist orderly arrived from	83

WAR DIARY
INTELLIGENCE SUMMARY.

Army Form C. 2118.

Hour, Date, Place	Summary of Events and Information	Remarks and references to Appendices
NOVEMBER 1914		
14th Cont'd LES LOBES	CAPT WARD reported No. 3rd Coy had been under heavy shrapnel fire that there had been several casualties – 1 killed (Pte F.J. MILNE) 10 wounded. Capt COLE also reported 1 man hit by shrapnel. Happens the shrapnel burst on the parapet of the trench & did most of the damage	C1
15th	Sent M? GIBSON party for MILNE's body. He arrived about 12.90 noon. We buried him at 3.30 pm in a garden opposite the farm where we were billeted. The C.O. read the service & No 3 Coy M?Oro attended. No. 1st Coy under Major COOPER went to CROIX BERSÉE entrenching again. Orders received to march at day break on BAILLEUL tomorrow.	C1 H.A.6
16th	Left LES LOBES at 6.45 a.m. – raining hard	

WAR DIARY
or
INTELLIGENCE SUMMARY.
(Erase heading not required.)

Army Form C. 2118.

Hour, Date, Place	Summary of Events and Information	Remarks and references to Appendices
NOVEMBER 1914		
16th Gntr LES LOBES 16	and very cold. arrived BAILLEUL 2 p.m - roads bad - disgusting march	13
17th 1st BAILLEUL	The C.O. met General Sir HORACE SMITH-DORRIEN who said he hoped to inspect the Battalion in a day or two. The C.O. went out to NEUVE EGLISE & watched the shelling of both sides. Many hostile aeroplanes about. The E.O. also met General CHETWODE and the Colonel of the Scots Greys - the latter gave him many useful tips about trench-work & advised him to get Regimental Telephones. Wired O.C. Depot for latter same night.	14
18th 1st BAILLEUL	LONDON RIFLE BRIGADE arrived - Colonel BRIDGWATER paid us a visit.	15
19th do	Route march for the Battalion - Snow fall	16
20th do	Route march for the Battalion - Received orders "Baths would move at 9.30 am tomorrow	17

Army Form C. 2118.

WAR DIARY
INTELLIGENCE SUMMARY.
(Erase heading not required.)

Hour, Date, Place		Summary of Events and Information	Remarks and references to Appendices
1914			
20th Oct	BAILLEUL	to NEUVE EGLISE & GENERAL SIR HORACE SMITH-DORRIEN rowed inspect us at 9.15 am. The QUEEN VICTORIA RIFLES arrived.	C1
21st	BAILLEUL to NEUVE EGLISE	GENERAL SIR HORACE SMITH-DORRIEN inspected the Battn & addressed us for 20 minutes. He said he was very glad to have such a fine reinforcement to his Corps. Trenched to billets at NEUVE EGLISE. CAPTAIN WALSH (Somerset L.I.) arrived, stating he was appointed adjutant of the Bttn. Then C.O. had no notification of this & CAPTAIN WALSH returned to BAILLEUL to await authority. MAJOR COOPER & No 1 Coy went into fire trenches attached to 4/ Middlesex.	C1
22nd	NEUVE EGLISE	CAPTAIN WALSH returned & took over adjutancy under authority from G.H.Q. No. 3 & 4 Coys went into front line trenches &7m Sg WULVERGHEM.	C1

WAR DIARY
or
INTELLIGENCE SUMMARY.
(Erase heading not required.)

Army Form C. 2118.

Hour, Date, Place	Summary of Events and Information	Remarks and references to Appendices
1914 NOVEMBER		
22nd and 23rd NEUVE EGLISE	They were heavily shelled on the way. No 1 Coy returned to NEUVE EGLISE.	[1]
23rd do	Quiet day	[1]
24th do	No 4 Coy relieved No 2 Coy at 4 am & the MIDDLESEX REGT relieved No 3 Coy at the same time [Both Companies returned to Hypo by 7pm. Casualties — Pte WILKINSON A.D.L. No 2 Coy slight gunshot wound scalp.]	[1]
25th do	No 1 Coy relieved No 4 Coy at 4 am in fire trenches — [No 4 returned to Bath Hypo 7am. Casualties; Pte MARSH — Severe head wound & Pte STAGG shot through Motor rifle. H.R.H. the PRINCE of WALES visited NEUVE EGLISE. GENERAL SIR HORACE SMITH DORRIEN visited our mess & chatted with the officers.]	[1]
26th do	No 1 Coy relieved by No 3 Coy at dawn. Casualties	

WAR DIARY
INTELLIGENCE SUMMARY.
(Erase heading not required.)

Army Form C. 2118.

27

Hour, Date, Place	Summary of Events and Information	Remarks and references to Appendices
NOVEMBER 1914		
26th Contd NEUVE EGLISE	SGT. THOMAS & PTES WEBSTER & A.V. JONES all No1 Coy killed. The two former were buried in front of the R/Scots H.qrs at WULVERGHEM & the latter in rear of the fire trench.	E1
27th do	No 2 Coy relieved No 3 Coy at dawn - Received orders to leave for WESTOUTRE at 3.15 p.m. Nos 1, 3 & 4 Coys marched off at that time to No 2 Coy followed with 2/R.Scots. Went into billets	E1 H.A.
28th & 29th do WESTOUTRE	Rested at WESTOUTRE. Voluntary Communion Parade on SUNDAY 29th - Over 300 men attended.	E1
30th do	Left at 4.30 for SHERPENBERG went into billets	E1
1st DECEMBER do 4/6 SHERPENBERG	H.qrs hut there - fine position - good view of battle line - first view of YPRES. Remained in billets	E1

7th Infantry Bde.
3rd Division.

HONOURABLE ARTILLERY COMPANY

DECEMBER 1914

(Joined 7th Bde. 8.12.14 from 8th Bde.)

HAC

WAR DIARY
or
INTELLIGENCE SUMMARY.
(Erase heading not required.)

Army Form C. 2118.

28

Hour, Date, Place	Summary of Events and Information	Remarks and references to Appendices
DECEMBER 1914 1st 2nd SHERPENBERG	Remained in billets. The C.O. went to the 8th Bde to arrange taking over the trenches. Major Harvon went on leave	H.A.C.
3rd do	A "red letter day". The British Monarch is with his army in the field for the first time for 170 years. His MAJESTY arrived outside No 3 billet at 1.45 pm accompanied by GENERAL SIR HORACE SMITH-DORRIEN - 2nd CORPS Commander, GENERAL HALDANE - 3rd DIVISION Commander - GENERAL BOWES - BRIGADIER 8th Brigade & many others. The Batn was drawn up in line facing the billets & as HIS MAJESTY paced each company he was given the H.A.C. Artillery fire. His MAJESTY addressed the C.O. - "Colonel TREFFRY, we meet under rather different auspices to those under which I had the pleasure of inspecting the H.A.C in LONDON." He then inspected the draw ruts the C.O introduced CAPTAIN WARD with	

WAR DIARY
or
~~INTELLIGENCE SUMMARY.~~
(*Erase heading not required.*)

Army Form C. 2118.

29

Hour, Date, Place	Summary of Events and Information	Remarks and references to Appendices
DECEMBER 1914 3rd Contd. SHERPENBERG	whom HIS MAJESTY shook hands. HIS MAJESTY went into the Sgts' Hut & talked to the Sgts & the men in another hut. H.R.H. The PRINCE OF WALES also went into the huts where the inspection was over. The C.O accompanied HIS MAJESTY to the road & in reply to HIS MAJESTY's enquiries informed him as to the number of casualties. HIS MAJESTY expressed his great pleasure that the men looked so well. He then shook hands with the C.O said "Well Colonel, I am delighted to have had a look at my Batln again under active conditions & I am very glad your casualties are so slight – I am informed the H.A.C is doing extremely well & that your General is very pleased with you. I shall continue to watch your doings with the greatest interest & wish you all every possible luck". The C.O thanked HIS MAJESTY & he again	

WAR DIARY
or
INTELLIGENCE SUMMARY.
(Erase heading not required.)

Army Form C. 2118.
30

Hour, Date, Place	Summary of Events and Information	Remarks and references to Appendices
DECEMBER 1914		
3rd contd SHERPENBERG	shot Lando. He then entered his car & drove off.	by H.M.
& KEMMEL	Immediately after the inspection the Battn marched to the trenches E. of KEMMEL. No 2 & 3 Companies were in BRIGADE Reserve were billeted in an old farm house.	[S]
4th KEMMEL	Kept quiet owning to hostile aeroplanes. [GENERAL SIR HORACE SMITH-DORRIEN GENERAL HALDANE visited our Headquarters.] Nos 2 & 3 Companies employed making dug-outs at night.	H.A.L [S]
5th do	Quiet day again - same Companies continued digging dug-outs at night.	[S]
6th do	Fine morning - Hostile aeroplanes very active. At 5.30 p.m. we were relieved by the LIVERPOOL SCOTTISH and marched to WESTOUTRE. [Journey on reaching there our billets were 1½ miles further on - most disappointing - everyone wet, cold & tired	[S]

WAR DIARY
or
INTELLIGENCE SUMMARY.

Army Form C. 2118.

31.

(Erase heading not required.)

Hour, Date, Place	Summary of Events and Information	Remarks and references to Appendices
DECEMBER 1914		
6th Contd KEMMEL to WESTOUTRE	Arrived in billets about 9.45 p.m. — No. 1 & 4 Coys arrived about 1 a.m. very exhausted. Heard Corpl FABIAN was killed last night & Pte BRAMMALL wounded — both No 1 Coy.	[1]
7th WESTOUTRE	Still very wet. The C.O. visited all billets received information that we were to be transferred to 7th BRIGADE.	[1] M.P.S.
8th do	Seventeen men returned who were left behind in the trenches. The C.O. visited 7th BRIGADE H.qrs & had an interview with the BRIGADIER. We are to take over a position of defence as a Battn for the first time. No 2 & 3 Companies to go into the firing line. No 1 & 4 in support Reserve.	[1]
9th WESTOUTRE to KEMMEL	Raining again. MAJOR HANSON returned from leave. Left billets 1.30 p.m. went via LACLYTTE to KEMMEL — rationed the Companies who were	[1]

WAR DIARY
or
INTELLIGENCE SUMMARY.
(Erase heading not required.)

Army Form C. 2118.

32

Hour, Date, Place	Summary of Events and Information	Remarks and references to Appendices
DECEMBER 1914		
9th and 10th KEMMEL	Going into fire trenches en route. MAJOR HANSON with CAPTAIN WALSH (ADJUTANT) No 2 & 3 Companies. Machine Gun Section & 50 men each from Nos 1 & 4 Companies proceeded to the trenches kholce a section on the Right Flank of the Brigade almost due E of KEMMEL. The Col took remainder of the Batt to the old farm house where they relieved the LIVERPOOL SCOTTISH	G1 H.H.L
10th do	Making fascines & collecting hurdles & planks for the trenches. Thought they were for us but they were unfortunately Commandeered for the ROYAL IRISH RIFLES. Heavy shelling all day. Casualties: Pte. C.S. SMALLMAN killed No 3 Coy & Pte HOLLINS No 1 Coy Wounded.	S1.
11th do	Parties continued making fascines etc. Very surprised these from BRIGADE Hqrs we shall	S1.

WAR DIARY or INTELLIGENCE SUMMARY

Army Form C. 2118.

33.

Hour, Date, Place	Summary of Events and Information	Remarks and references to Appendices
DECEMBER 1914 11th Cont'd KEMMEL	not be relieved until tomorrow. Casualties: Pte A.D. Paul No 1 Coy killed.	
12th do	The C.O. visited Captain Walsh at Ammunition Farm. Found him very unwell - Captain White + 2/Lt Gibson came in. In the morning Pte White hardly stagger. The C.O. arranged for him to be revived at Kemmel as the crew wound he no wet - Weather awful. Heard Pte Paul was buried by a party under Sgt Major Atkins + that he was hit whilst taking up rations. The C.O. sent all men at the Ferme Hance Brocre as soon as the Royal Scots Fus'rs arrived Releive them. The men from the trenches arrived at Kemmel at 10 p.m. [When the hot tea was much appreciated.] The party then proceeded Brocre, + went into billets between 11 p.m. 12 p.m.	S.1 N.A. S.1

WAR DIARY
or
INTELLIGENCE SUMMARY.
(Erase heading not required.)

Army Form C. 2118.

34

Hour, Date, Place	Summary of Events and Information	Remarks and references to Appendices
DECEMBER 1914 13th LOCRE	Said me have many sick, CAPTAIN WALSH (ADJT), CAPTAIN WHYTE, 2/Lt GIBSON, 2nd Lt. BOWER, LIEUT CARNWATH (M.O.) amongst them. Machine Gun Section under 2/Lt HOLLIDAY was brigaded returned to KEMMEL to support an attack by the 8th BRIGADE	E.J
14th do	In billets – Machine Gun Section reported to have done very well in the attack. Casualties CPL McGOWAN, PTES MACNAMARA, TRAVERS & LAWDEN all wounded.	E.J
15th do KEMMEL	CAPTAIN WALSH, CAPTAIN WHYTE, LIEUT CARNWATH, & 2nd Lieuts BYRON, GIBSON & BOWER all went to hospital also some 50 men. The Battn returned to the same trenches at KEMMEL Relieved the ROYAL SCOTS FUSR'S. No 1 & No 4 Coys went into the fire trenches & No's 2 & 3 Companies in Reserve. The signallers laid telephone wire from Battn Hqrs at KEMMEL to the fire trenches. Casualties Pte KRAY No 1 Coy wounded.	E.J H.A.C

WAR DIARY
or
INTELLIGENCE SUMMARY.
(Erase heading not required.)

Army Form C. 2118.

35

Hour, Date, Place		Summary of Events and Information	Remarks and references to Appendices
DECEMBER 1914			
16th	KEMMEL	Quiet night. Battn HQrs shelled in the afternoon with Jack Johnsons & shrapnel — all turned out & took cover in dugouts for an hour or so. The phone wires destroyed by shelling — They were repaired by the Signallers after dark.	S.1
17th	do	Quiet day — [Pte BRENNAN] wounded.	S.1
18th	do	[Corpl TATE] killed. 5.30 pm. 1/Gordons arrived to relieve us — They took 6 hours to do it so the C.O. did not get back to LOCRE till 2 am.	S.1
19th	LOCRE	In billets. Xmas mail arrived.	S.1 H.A.C.
20th	do	In billets: Holy Communion at 8 am. Church of England Service at 11 am. 46 him Major COOPER & LIEUT DOBSON went on leave.	S.1
21st	do	In billets: [LIEUT GARRETT went to BRIGADE HQrs for duty.]	S.1
22nd	do	In billets.	S.1
23rd	do	Church of England Service at 6 p.m.	S.1
24th	do	H.C. Service 6, 7 & 8 am — 250 four our men attended.	S.1

Army Form C. 2118.

WAR DIARY
or
INTELLIGENCE SUMMARY.   36.
(Erase heading not required.)

Hour, Date, Place	Summary of Events and Information	Remarks and references to Appendices
DECEMBER 1914		
24th contd LOCRE to KEMMEL	Left for KEMMEL at 3.45 p.m. relieved the Royal Scots Fus' there. Relief completed at 8.30 p.m. Very sharp frost.	E.1
25th KEMMEL	Under cover of a fog the C.O. visited fire trench F2 with CAPTAIN WARD as guide & CAPTAIN DOUGLASH. Saw CAPTAIN NEWTON & LT PERKINS there.	E.1
26th do	Carried out our own relief at 5 a.m. - all well. Sgt DALE (No1 Coy) killed during the day & Corpl S.E. JOHNSON wounded in the head.	E.1
27th do to WESTOUTRE	All quiet in the trenches during the day. 2/Suffolks relieved us - completed at 8 p.m. Marched to WESTOUTRE from trenches - last party & C.O arrived in billets at 12 midnight.	E.1 L.A. 6
28th - 29th & 30th & 31st WESTOUTRE	In billets at WESTOUTRE.	E.3

7th Inf.Bde.
3rd Div.

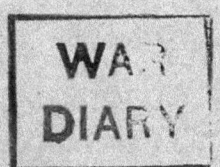

1st BATTN. THE HONOURABLE ARTILLERY COMPANY.

J A N U A R Y

1 9 1 5

WAR DIARY or INTELLIGENCE SUMMARY.

(Erase heading not required.)

Army Form C. 2118.

Hour, Date, Place	Summary of Events and Information	Remarks and references to Appendices
JANUARY 1st 1915. 2nd LOCRE.	Arrive in Billets at LOCRE from WESTOUTRE. Billets LOCRE. Party of N.C.O's and men receiving instructions in the throwing of hand-grenades	
3rd do.	Billets LOCRE.	
4th do.	Left LOCRE at 4-15 A.M. for the trenches. Nos 1 and 4 Companies went in, relieving the Royal Fusiliers and Royal Scots Fusiliers. Nos 2 and 3 Companies went into billets at KEMMEL.	
5th KEMMEL.	All well at the trenches. C.O. and Major Cooper reconnoitred the trenches from a haystack E of LINDENHOEK about 1000 yds in the rear of the trenches. All German trenches in front of SPANBROEK-FARM clearly visible.	
6th do.	Captain Newton killed 9 A.M. and 3 men wounded by enfilade fire of Machine Gun in F.I. trench	
7th do.	All quiet in the trenches. 2nd Lt MURNANE appointed Brigade Pioneer Officer, his duties being to direct the making of wire entanglements, fascines c/o for general protection.	

WAR DIARY or **INTELLIGENCE SUMMARY**

Army Form C. 2118.
38/.

(Erase heading not required.)

Instructions regarding War Diaries and Intelligence Summaries are contained in F. S. Regs., Part II. and the Staff Manual respectively. Title pages will be prepared in manuscript.

Hour, Date, Place	Summary of Events and Information	Remarks and references to Appendices
JAN. 8th KEMMEL	All quiet in the trenches, relieved by Royal Fusiliers & Royal Scots Fusiliers & Liverpool Scottish Regiments. Arrived back in LOCRE about 11 P.M. Captains Ward and Meaham go on leave to England	
do. 9th LOCRE.	Billets LOCRE.	
10th do	Billets LOCRE. Lieut Perkins sent down for a rest, suffering from a nervous breakdown.	
11th do	Billets LOCRE	
12th do	Left for the trenches at 4-15 P.M. Nos 2 and 3 Companies went into the trenches	
13th KEMMEL	Private Stone No 3 Company killed. Draft arrived under charge of Lieut Ellis, total 280 men. 2nd Lieutenants Stone, Brunton & Sturges also arrived with this draft. All quiet in the trenches. Draft take up fascines, etc for the trenches at night	
14th do.		
15th do.	Ditto for 14th.	

WAR DIARY
or
INTELLIGENCE SUMMARY.
(Erase heading not required.)

Army Form C. 2118.

Hour, Date, Place	Summary of Events and Information	Remarks and references to Appendices
JAN. 16th KEMMEL.	Battalion relieved. Conference in the trenches relieved by the Royal Fusiliers and Royal Scots Fusiliers. Capt Garnsey, Capt Collum & the C.O. left LOCRE at midnight for England on leave	
17th LOCRE.	Major Cooper acting for C.O. during his leave of absence. In Billets LOCRE.	
18th do.	Inspection of the Rifles of the draft carried out.	
19th do	Billets LOCRE. Inoculation proceeded with.	
20th do	Left LOCRE for KEMMEL at 4-15pm to relieve the 9th Brigade	
21st KEMMEL	Major Cooper went to Hospital, Capt Ward took over command	
22nd do	Capt/Lieut Chittick killed in the trenches	
23rd do.	All quiet in the trenches - SPANBROEK FARM shelled.	

WAR DIARY
or
INTELLIGENCE SUMMARY.
(Erase heading not required.)

Army Form C. 2118.

Hour, Date, Place		Summary of Events and Information	Remarks and references to Appendices
JAN. 24	KEMMEL	Battalion relieved by the 9th Brigade in the trenches. C.O. and Captain Gairnsey and Lt Collins returned from leave.	
25	LOCRE.	Billets LOCRE. Capt Dougan & Lt Murnane to London on leave	
26	do.	Billets. LOCRE.	
27	do.	— do —	
28	do.	Battalion proceed to the trenches. Half of No 1 Coy and half of No 2 went in, and 50 of No 2. Company. Battalion Headquarters at the Chalet. KEMMEL much more comfortable. Pte KIDD No 2 Coy wounded.	
29	KEMMEL.	KEMMEL shelled at 2-30 p.m. 9 S. LANCS killed and 15 wounded. Pte Johnston No 1 Company wounded.	

WAR DIARY
or
INTELLIGENCE SUMMARY.

(Erase heading not required.)

Army Form C. 2118.

Hour, Date, Place	Summary of Events and Information	Remarks and references to Appendices
JAN. 30 KEMMEL.	Sergeant Dowett No-2 Coy killed, and Private Drysdale No-3 Coy killed.	41/
31 do.	Quiet day in the trenches.	

7th Inf.Bde.
3rd Div.

(Battn. attached to
85th Inf.Bde. 28th
Div. 20.2.15 - 4.4.15)

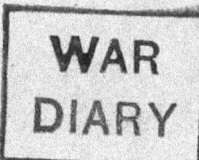

1st BATTN. THE HONOURABLE ARTILLERY COMPANY.

F E B R U A R Y

1 9 1 5

WAR DIARY
INTELLIGENCE SUMMARY
(Erase heading not required.)

Army Form C. 2118.

Hour, Date, Place	Summary of Events and Information	Remarks and references to Appendices
FEBRUARY. 1.	Very quiet day. Relieved by Royal Fusiliers and Royal Scots Fusiliers. L/Cpl Scott No 1 Coy.] slightly wounded. Return to billets at LOCRE. The rain was very dry and a good deal of work was got through.	
2.	Billets LOCRE. [Capt Lambert & Lt. Osmond go on leave to England. Capt Douglas Lt Murnane returned	H.H.
3.	Billets LOCRE.	
4.	— do —	
5.	Battalion leaves LOCRE for the trenches, and relieves Royal Scots Fusiliers & Royal Fusiliers in F sector. F 2 taken over by the Worcesters. We have held F.2 since Nov 19th & Took over part of F.3 instead. Battn Headquarters at the Chalet. Men billeted in farms around LINDENHOEK.	1 Dec.
6.	Quiet day. C.O. nsited LINDENHOEK billets. Order to take over a sector from 4th Middlesex and to hand over F sector to the Worcesters. Pink Kempenel No 4 Coy relieved No 2 & 3 Coy relieve Middlesex in F.1,2 & S.5. etc.	
	(continued)	

WAR DIARY or INTELLIGENCE SUMMARY.

Army Form C. 2118.

Hour, Date, Place	Summary of Events and Information	Remarks and references to Appendices
FEBRUARY. 7th (cont.)	Pronato, Thompson & Aske wounded, otherwise the Coy. carried out a Guy Fkes. However late in the evening Sector. B. Coy. not so confident midnight. [Private Leslin, Machine gunner wounded.] Pvt Lanyard buried in the back ground. Kemmel. Took all our Headquarters on the KEMMEL – VIERSTRAAT road	
8.	All well on all sector. Saw several wounded in front. 2nd Lt Jones & 2nd Lt Adams wounded.	
9.	All quiet in trenches. C.O. visited Suffolk's Signal Corp'n on our left. 2nd Lt Shortworthy badly. Relieved by Royal Fusiliers and returned to Billets at LOCRE.	
10.	Billets LOCRE	
11.	do	
12.	do	
13.	do [Capt Holt (Adjutant) & Lt R.T.F.) Adjutant, returned to duty, also Lt Garneau, both from sick leave in England. We relieve the Royal Fusiliers in trenches, rebg. confident 6. 9-30 p.m. All well. C.O. Royal Fusiliers informed C.O. that the Enemy had been cooking during the day & that we should probably be relieved to-morrow.]	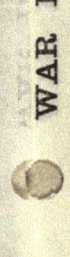

WAR DIARY or INTELLIGENCE SUMMARY

Army Form C. 2118.

Hour, Date, Place	Summary of Events and Information	Remarks and references to Appendices
FEBRUARY. 14.	All quiet during night. R.E.'s working on S.S. Redoubt. Neighbourhood of Batt. Headquarters shelled during the day. Fine weather.	
15.	All well during the night. Artillery fire kept up all night, one Gun evidently suffering Division on our left. Enemy commence shelling Redoubt at 7 A.M. Heavy Battery fire & several tornados and shelling ceased at 2.15 P.M. Capt Ward reported K2 being heavily shelled and thought blown in. His RSM. he had severeral Casualties. Heavy Batty opened fire on the trench in front of K.2. 7. P.M. Capt Ward reported that as result of enemy's shelling, one killed seventeen wounded (including himself). 9 P.M. Reported north of cottage men's dugouts were becoming had fate, in enemy's 23 men all however were got out, and only 9 found to be badly hurt. All damage to K.2 repaired during the night.	H.A.C.
16.	Quiet during the day.	
17.	Brenan [Holman] killed at Jug R. While on way over billets. Heard from Brigade Office that we should not be relieved for some days prior to the 9th Brigade being moved North W.R. at Ouzell [Wadi] wounded.	

WAR DIARY or INTELLIGENCE SUMMARY

Army Form C. 2118.

Hour, Date, Place	Summary of Events and Information	Remarks and references to Appendices
FEBRUARY 1915. 18th	All quiet during night. [Head K.Powell died in Field Ambulance and was buried in LOCRE church yard this morning] Eept Hazel and the C.O visited S.5. Great deal of footing going on.	
19.	All well in trenches. Continuous firing all night. Ordered to return to LOCRE relieved by Worhs and Gordons and to report to the 85th Infantry Brigade, to whom we are to be attached for the time being. [Everyone sorry to leave the Brigade, though we shall soon return.] 7th Brigade. Report to G.O.C. 85th Brigade	A.P. 6.
20.	Billets LOCRE.	
21.	Billets LOCRE.	
22.	Leave LOCRE for the trenches to relieve the Worcesters in the F. sector. Take over F.2.3.4.5.6 and S.2. Billeted in KEMMEL and LINDENHOEK.	
23.	All well in trenches, which have been much improved. Private Peacock Landle No 1 Co killed in F.2 trench.	
24.	Quiet night, good deal of shelling from Field Guns during the day.	

Army Form C. 2118.

WAR DIARY
or
INTELLIGENCE SUMMARY.
(Erase heading not required.)

Instructions regarding War Diaries and Intelligence Summaries are contained in F.S. Regs., Part II. and the Staff Manual respectively. Title pages will be prepared in manuscript.

Hour, Date, Place	Summary of Events and Information	Remarks and references to Appendices
FEBRUARY 25.	All quiet during the night on our front, but continuous firing on our left. Private Leroy killed. Cor Harral badly wounded. Corporals Conway & Duedin [wounded].	
26.	All quiet during the day. Relieved by Worcesters, South Lancs, and returned to Billets at LOC R.E.	
27.	Billets LOC R.E.	
28.	— do. —	

7th Inf.Bde.
3rd Div.

(Battn attached to
85th Inf.Bde. 28th
Div. 20.2.15 to
4.4.15).

WAR DIARY

1st BATTN. THE HONOURABLE ARTILLERY COMPANY.

M A R C H

1 9 1 5

Army Form C. 2118.

WAR DIARY or INTELLIGENCE SUMMARY.
(Erase heading not required.)

Hour, Date, Place	Summary of Events and Information	Remarks and references to Appendices
MARCH 1st LOCRE	In Billets. Gen. Sir H. SMITH DORRIEN [Commanding 2nd ARMY] visited H.Q. HAC [and had a long conversation with the C.O. and Officers]. He said he had come personally to congratulate the Battalion on the work it had done and the name it had made for itself.	
2nd LOCRE	In billets.	
3rd "		
4th "	Relieved the S. Lancs and the Worcesters in F Sector trenches and S2 & S3 — 400 men in trenches. Relief effected without loss.	
5th KEMMEL	In trenches. [C.O. visited S3 with H.Q. on Ward.] Several casualties during relief on WYTSCHAETE Rd which is becoming very unhealthy. [2/Lt R J DRURY, Pts G N GRAYBURN, E C R PEBERDY, H B VINEY, F H D CLAUDET.]

Army Form C. 2118.

INTELLIGENCE SUMMARY.
(Erase heading not required.)

Hour, Date, Place	Summary of Events and Information	Remarks and references to Appendices
MARCH 5th (cont?)	of No 1 Cy A.J CRAIGY. No 3 Cy wounded.	
6th KEMMEL	In trenches. have casualties in WYTSCHAETE. R¹ during relief — needed to change time of reliefs. Pte M.G. JANESON. No 1 Cy killed. Pte R.E NICKELS. No 1 Cy wounded. + Pte W.E. BIFFEN. No 2 Cy.	
7th KEMMEL	In trenches — did not to relieve till 1 A.M. owing to firing. [Ptes H.B. BELDER. No 2 (MG) E.H LINDEMAN No 1.(MG) and R.J FOWLES No 1. wounded.]	
8th KEMMEL	In trenches. Reliefs better. no casualties. men upon 48 hours to minimise risk of casualties. Bombardment of SPANBROEK MOLEN — no visible damage [Corpl KINGSLEY SMITH No 2 Cy wounded.]	
9th KEMMEL	In trenches. Renewed bomb¹ of SPANBROEK MOLEN. Some length of enemy wire damaged. [L/cpl P.C. HOYLAND No 4. + Cpl C.H. STOCK wounded. The latter No 3 Cy.]	

INTELLIGENCE SUMMARY.

(Erase heading not required.)

Army Form C. 2118.

Instructions regarding War Diaries and Intelligence Summaries are contained in F.S. Regs., Part II. and the Staff Manual respectively. Title pages will be prepared in manuscript.

Hour, Date, Place	Summary of Events and Information	Remarks and references to Appendices
MARCH. 10th KEMMEL	In trenches. Relief effected last night at 2 A.M. all well. No casualties. Renewed bombt of SPANBROEK. [Recvd news that we have gained a success at NEUVE CHAPELLE]	
11th KEMMEL	In trenches. French patrols kept up constant fire on enemys damaged wire and parapet during night. News that NEUVE CHAPELLE affair much bigger than at 1st thought. Hear that 50 Battalions took part. that we gained about 2 miles of ground over a 2½ mile front, about 2000 prisoners taken and enemys casualties reputed to be at least 17,000. Our losses 12,000. Casualties Pte A.C. PARRY and J.L.ENSISLE No 1 Coy killed. Pte W.G. NORTON 1 Coy wounded	
12th KEMMEL	In trenches. Orders for all trenches to be ready to support an attack on SPANBROEK MOLEN by the 7th Infantry Brigade to start at 7.40. During	

INTELLIGENCE SUMMARY.

(Erase heading not required.)

Hour, Date, Place	Summary of Events and Information	Remarks and references to Appendices
	to not attacked till 4.10 P.M. Heavy bombardment of mill and trenches at 3 P.M. Attack by the WILTS and WORCESTERS at 4.10 P.M. which failed. Losses about 19 Officers and 300-400 men. We did our best with machine guns and rifle grenades to support the attack. The attack failed tho' the machine gun emplacements of the enemy not having been destroyed by our artillery, — 3 of the emplacements had been pointed out to higher authorities on several occasions previous to the attack. We lost 3 killed in F 4. [Dev S.C. LINDSEY, C.GOODMAN 3 Coy. L. INSKIPP. 4 Coy.] Wounded. [P.G. S.H. MORGAN, C.R FOWLER, T.H FOWLER. 3 Coy. H.A. RYAN, 2 Coy and R.T. HUNTER 4 Coy.]	
13th KEMMEL	In trenches. Last night all standing to expecting counter attack but nothing happened. Our trenches F4 particularly shelled during day. Casualties	

INTELLIGENCE SUMMARY.

(Erase heading not required.)

Hour, Date, Place	Summary of Events and Information	Remarks and references to Appendices
MARCH 13th (cont d) KEMMEL	Sergt POSTLETHWAITE L/Cpl GR EDDIE Pte H.F. WHITMORE, E.R. CIMBER, W.H. BURDETT. G.F. SADLER. T.H. MCILWRAITH. 3 Coy. Jns JOHNSTONE + R.H. CROSS 2 Coy. wounded.	
14th KEMMEL	In trenches. Hope to be relieved tonight became very tired. About 5.30 heavy shell fire on our left. Several shells into KEMMEL. Heavy rifle and artillery fire in direction of ST ELOI. Heard later germans taken ST ELOI, lost trenches + wound. No relief tonight	Pte H. C. GOGG
15th KEMMEL	In trenches. Quiet day and night. B Coy wounded.	
16th KEMMEL	In trenches. Quiet. Relieved by 1st WILTS.REGT + 4th SOUTH LANCS. Proceeded to billets at WEST-OUTRE. Our largest stretch in trenches. Total casualties 8 killed 30 wounded. 10 days casualties Pte P.C. HOLLINGSWORTH A Coy. J.A. PRITCHARD C Coy. wound	

Army Form C. 2118.

INTELLIGENCE SUMMARY.
or
(Erase heading not required.)

Instructions regarding War Diaries and Intelligence Summaries are contained in F.S. Regs., Part II. and the Staff Manual respectively. Title pages will be prepared in manuscript.

Hour, Date, Place	Summary of Events and Information	Remarks and references to Appendices
MARCH 1915.		
17th KEMMEL to WESTOUTRE	In Billets	
18th WESTOUTRE	"	
19th WESTOUTRE	"	
20th WESTOUTRE	"	
21st WESTOUTRE	" (Change in weather, lovely day)	
22nd WESTOUTRE	" At 10 A.M. Officers & NCO's attended lecture and practical example of sapping at spot half way between LOCRE and WESTOUTRE. The C.O. Captain Ward. The Adjutant at 5 P.M. Company Officers attended conference at the Convent, LOCRE, on the subject of the new trenches which the Battalion are taking over to-morrow at ST ELOI. The C.O. Captain Ward. Captain January.	

Army Form C. 2118.

INTELLIGENCE SUMMARY.

(Erase heading not required.)

Instructions regarding War Diaries and Intelligence Summaries are contained in F. S. Regs., Part II. and the Staff Manual respectively. Title pages will be prepared in manuscript.

Hour, Date, Place	Summary of Events and Information	Remarks and references to Appendices
MARCH 22nd (Westoutre) Contd	Captain Boyle + Lieut Begin went to view the new position at ST. ELOI. Another very fine day.	
23rd WESTOUTRE	The Battalion paraded at 11 A.M. in field next to No. B. Coy Officers Billet. The C.O. addressed the Battalion on the subject of the new trenches which are to be taken over this evening. The Battalion left WESTOUTRE at 6 P.M. for ST ELOI and with a halt of 10 minutes reached DICKEBUSCH at 8.15. [via SCHERPENBERG, LA CLYTTE.] after a halt at DICKEBUSCH] moved on thro' KRUISSTRAAT HOEK + VOORMEZEELE into the trenches B + C in fire trenches A + D in support - the whole Batt'n with exception of a few wounded & sick who had fallen out on march being in the trenches at same time. Headquarters + details	

INTELLIGENCE SUMMARY.

(Erase heading not required.)

Army Form C. 2118.

Hour, Date, Place	Summary of Events and Information	Remarks and references to Appendices
MARCH 23rd Cont'd WESTOUTRE to ST ELOI	Being in cellars &c in ruined YDORMEZEELE. [Mr. WORSLEY was wounded in the leg getting into his trench.] Wet night eventually all settled down in billets about 2 A.M. The rest has much improved Co. WYTSCHAETE Rd — much healthier. [Casualties. Pte H.M. Parsons killed — Pte J.H. Lupton + J.D. Luton wounded. Also 6 company the late died of wounds March 26th buried at Bailleul]	
24 ST ELOI	Quiet during the day. A little intermittent shelling during the day — whiz bangs + trench mortar. Casualties in fire trenches from rifle fire: [Pte A.L. DAVIES, L/Cpl E.B. BUCKNEY killed. Pte L.J. FEARNLEY wounded all of C company.]	
25 " "	Intermittent shelling during day chiefly whiz bangs & trench mortar. Casualties. [Pte P. FITCH B. Coy] killed — [5 ptes] F.O. FORRESTER, H.C. BECKTON, O.W. THORNHILL + Cpl R. CRAMPTON all of C company + Pte C.C. KIELAN B Coy] 5 wounded. In evening A + D relieved B + C in fire	

Army Form C. 2118.

INTELLIGENCE SUMMARY.

(Erase heading not required.)

Hour, Date, Place	Summary of Events and Information	Remarks and references to Appendices
March.		
26th ST ELOI	trenches. [The C.O., Captain Ward and the Adjutant visited the trenches and went all round. A very wet day followed by frost at night.] A quiet day, very little doing in trenches.	
27th "	In trenches. Some shelling in whiz bangs in the afternoon. [Hear that we are going to be relieved by the Wiltshire Regiment.] Aeroplanes very active all day. We are relieved by the Wilts and go back for rest to huts beyond DICKEBUSCH. [Casualties Ptes H.H. LAST, B Coy & Fl. SHARPIN D Coy wounded.]	
28th DICKEBUSCH.	In huts here. Very nice situation. Fatigue party carrying material to trenches in evening.	
29th "	Still in huts. German aeroplanes very active but kept away by our shells. Parade at 9 P.M. to go into trenches again at ST ELOI where we relieve the	

Instructions regarding War Diaries and Intelligence Summaries are contained in F.S. Regs., Part II. and the Staff Manual respectively. Title pages will be prepared in manuscript.

Army Form C. 2118.

INTELLIGENCE SUMMARY.

(Erase heading not required.)

Hour, Date, Place	Summary of Events and Information	Remarks and references to Appendices
March.	Wiltshire regiment. Very fine weather continues but very cold.	
30th ST. ELOI.	In trenches - very quiet day. Germans shelling behind the trenches. One of the Snipers Pte E.B. DON B Coy wounded. A great deal of work put in on improving the trenches during the night and much wire put out.	
31st " "	In trenches - very quiet day. Germans of am heavy shelling behind also on YPRES. Fine weather still continues. The Batn. relieved in the evening by the WILTS. REGT and return again to the DICKEBUSCH huts.	

7th Inf.Bde.
3rd Div.

(Battn. attached
to 85th Inf.Bde.
28th Div.
20.2.15 to 4.4.15)

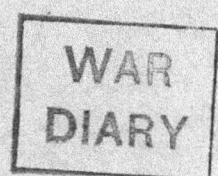

1st BATTN. THE HONOURABLE ARTILLERY COMPANY.

A P R I L

1 9 1 5

Army Form C. 2118.

WAR DIARY or INTELLIGENCE SUMMARY.   1/Honourable Artillery Company.

April 1915

(Erase heading not required.)

Instructions regarding War Diaries and Intelligence Summaries are contained in F. S. Regs., Part II. and the Staff Manual respectively. Title pages will be prepared in manuscript.

Place	Date	Hour	Summary of Events and Information	Remarks and references to Appendices
DICKEBUSCH	April 1st		In huts — lovely day. 250 of the Battalion went on fatigues in the evening. Carrying rations for the WILTS REG:T — Taking up barbed wire, sand bags &c. filling sand bags and making trenches round bge.	

WAR DIARY or INTELLIGENCE SUMMARY.

Army Form C. 2118.

(Erase heading not required.)

Hour, Date, Place		Summary of Events and Information	Remarks and references to Appendices
April 1st	DICKEBUSCH	Barricade etc at ST ELOI. Lieut HAYDEN was in charge.	
2nd	DICKEBUSCH	In huts - We [were] moved back to the 7th Brigade from the 85th [and the Battalion leave the huts at 6.45 PM and move] to Billets in DICKEBUSCH. The C.O., the Adjutant, Captains of companies and some Subalterns went up at 8.45. to see the new trenches which the Battalion are taking over on the night of ST ELOI and returned to DICKEBUSCH at about 1.A.M. next evening.	
3rd	DICKEBUSCH	In Billets - A fatigue party of 300 of the Battalion under Captain LANKESTER. paraded at R.E. Park at 10.45. for trench digging. and proceeded to the BRASSERIE ELZENWALLE when they were dismissed owing to bad weather & returned to DICKEBUSCH about 1.30. A.M.	

Army Form C. 2118.

WAR DIARY
or
INTELLIGENCE SUMMARY.
(Erase heading not required.)

Instructions regarding War Diaries and Intelligence Summaries are contained in F.S. Regs., Part II. and the Staff Manual respectively. Title pages will be prepared in manuscript.

Hour, Date, Place	Summary of Events and Information	Remarks and references to Appendices
April. 4th DICKEBUSCH Easter Sunday.	Wet morning - Services in the Hospital 6.30, 7, 7.30 and 8. The Battalion paraded at 7 P.M. and moved to ELZENWALLE Crossroads where met guides of the R.I.R. and took over the trenches P2, P2A, P3, P4, P4A, P4B, P5, P6, + S7 at ST.ELOI. B Company remained in the billets at the CHATEAU and at the Crossroads at ELZENWALLE. The C.O. and the Adjutant made their headquarters at NEW. FARM. Captain WARD and others. Officers billeted in the CHATEAU. Wet night. Casualties L/Sergt. E.HOYLE, A Coy killed - buried in the CHATEAU garden ELZENWALLE. L/Cpl A.F.SMALLMAN - Ptes H.G.MILNE +C.H.ROLFE wounded all of C.Coy	
5th ST ELOI	In the trenches. Quiet day. wet afternoon and evening. Pioneers working on the wire in front of P5 +P6. Water parties sent down to ELZENWALLE in evening. Casualties Pte H.E.Coomber D.Co.Y killed - buried in the CHATEAU garden ELZENWALLE.	

Army Form C. 2118.

WAR DIARY
INTELLIGENCE SUMMARY
(Erase heading not required.)

Instructions regarding War Diaries and Intelligence Summaries are contained in F.S. Regs., Part II. and the Staff Manual respectively. Title pages will be prepared in manuscript.

Hour, Date, Place	Summary of Events and Information	Remarks and references to Appendices
April 6th ST ELOI	In the trenches. Quiet day. Artillery fairly busy also Aeroplanes, a few whiz bangs at trenches. In the evening the Companies changed over A Coy & B Coy to fire trenches D in support + redoubt. C went to close billets at Chateau. A very wet and dark night, the changes were all effected by 4 A.M. without any casualties - Everyone wet through. One casualty during day. Pte E CANKELL D.Coy wounded.	
7th ST ELOI	In the trenches. Fine morning. Quiet day. Water and ration parties went down to Crossroads in evening — Casualties. Pte W EVANS A Coy. wounded.	
8th ST ELOI	In the trenches. Showery morning. Fine afternoon + evening Quiet day. a little shelling. The Wiltshire Regiment relieved us in the evening. our guides met them at ELZENWALLE Cross roads at 8 P.M. The last company reached DICKEBUSCH at about 1.30 A.M. Scene billets as last time	

Army Form C. 2118.

WAR DIARY
or
INTELLIGENCE SUMMARY.
(Erase heading not required.)

Hour, Date, Place	Summary of Events and Information	Remarks and references to Appendices
April 9th DICKEBUSCH	In billets. Thunderstorm with snow in the morning. Heavy cannonade all the afternoon and evening to the North. 20% leave given to NCO's and men.	
10th DICKEBUSCH	In billets. 20% leave given to NCO's and men. Fatigue parties in the evening. 120 carrying stores and materials to trenches under Captain HOLLIDAY and Mr. REED. 200 digging behind P2. with Capt. BOYLE. Mr. McARTHUR and Mr. CANNING. Fine day.	
11th DICKEBUSCH	Some shells over DICKEBUSCH in the morning, shrapnel. Turned into 20% leave given to NCO's & men. Fatigue parties in the evening. 100 carrying materials, corrugated iron, stakes &c. to S.8. (formerly 57) under Mr Blake. 200 digging from road behind S.8. towards ELZENWALLE with Captain HAYDEN. Mr TATHAM and Mr MONTAGU. Fine day.	

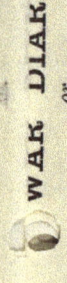

WAR DIARY or INTELLIGENCE SUMMARY.

(Erase heading not required.)

Army Form C. 2118.

Instructions regarding War Diaries and Intelligence Summaries are contained in F.S. Regs., Part II. and the Staff Manual respectively. Title pages will be prepared in manuscript.

Hour, Date, Place	Summary of Events and Information	Remarks and references to Appendices
APRIL 12th DICKEBUSCH	In Billets. The Battalion paraded at 7.30 and moved to ELZENWALLE cross Roads to relieve the WILTSHIRE. Regt in the same trenches as before. A Coy to close billets in the CHATEAU. B Coy. C Coy. P2 + P3. D Coy. the CO + Adjutant moved Headquarters from New farm to Casualty. Pte R WILLIAMS B Coy Machine gun Section killed. buried at the CHATEAU 13.4.15. Fine day. During the night a Zeppelin passed over our lines towards DICKEBUSCH - it passed over the CHATEAU at 11.50 being seen by the sentry.	
13th ST ELOI	Quiet day in the trenches. Casualties — Sgt S.D ALLEN D Coy killed. L/Cpl R.F. KENT. B Coy and Pte E.S. Brass B Coy wounded. Fatigue parties of A Coy taking lore etc to trenches in evening.	
14th ST ELOI.	Quiet day in trenches. The companies changed over	

WAR DIARY or INTELLIGENCE SUMMARY

Army Form C. 2118.

Hour, Date, Place	Summary of Events and Information	Remarks and references to Appendices
APRIL 14th (Contd)	In Evening "A" Coy going to P.2 and P.3. "B" Coy came in after.	
17th DICKEBUSCH 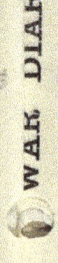	Casualties. Pte G.S. GRUNDY. A Coy killed. Pte C. Turner A Coy. T.E. HULME and T.L.G. TURNBULL B Coy wounded. The last died of wounds 15.4.15. buried at DICKEBUSCH. At 11.15 P.M. a heavy rifle fire started also artillery and a mine was exploded by the Germans under French P.1. But there was not an attack and everything quieted down in about an hour.	
15th ST ELOI	Quiet day in the Trenches. Fine day. Casualty. 2nd Cpl. G.R. WHITE A Coy wounded	
16th ST ELOI	Quiet day in the trenches. The German Artillery fairly busy in the afternoon, all sorts. Aeroplanes also busy. At about 10 - 10.30 we were relieved by the	

WAR DIARY or INTELLIGENCE SUMMARY.

Army Form C. 2118.

Hour, Date, Place	Summary of Events and Information	Remarks and references to Appendices
APRIL 16th Cont.	WILTS. REGT and returned to billets in DICKEBUSCH. Same as before. 1st and coy getting in at about 12.30 A.M. A fine day followed by a very wet night.	
17th DICKEBUSCH	In Billets. Left half Battalion stood to from 6 P.M. to 6 P.M. 18th. A heavy bombardment started at about 7 P.M. on the left. our batteries shelling the German position and an attack was made on Hill 60. ZILLEBEKE The bombardment continued during the night.	
18th DICKEBUSCH	In Billets. We hear to-day that last night's attack was successful and that German counter attack early this morning was repulsed. The farm and but two by shells close to B. Coy Billet this morning. A fatigue party consisting of 100 men of A Coy with Mr SCHIFF and Mr REED paraded at 7 P.M. for digging a similar number from B Coy with	

Army Form C. 2118.

INTELLIGENCE SUMMARY.

(Erase heading not required.)

Instructions regarding War Diaries and Intelligence Summaries are contained in F.S. Regs., Part II. and the Staff Manual respectively. Title pages will be prepared in manuscript.

Hour, Date, Place	Summary of Events and Information	Remarks and references to Appendices
APRIL 19th DICKEBUSCH	In Billets. The Germans pressure by shells into the village at 12.45 for about 1/2 hour, near the hospital are patching into the South Lancs billet in the main street - all our men were got out into the fields at the back without any casualty. The South Lancs had 3 injured. Parties of 100 men from C. Coy [with Mr DAVIES and Mr STONE] and D Coy [with Mr MORPHY and Mr STURGESS under Captain COLLINS] went digging. A & B Coys stood to from 6 P.M. 19th to 6 P.M. 20th. The digging parties returned to DICKEBUSCH at about 11.30 P.M. Fine weather. 20% leave to NCOs + men.	
20th DICKEBUSCH	In Billets. The C.O. held a meeting with Captains of Companies at 12.30 P.M. with reference to teaching the evening. The Battalion paraded at 7.30 P.M. + marched to ELZENWALLE cross roads + the BRASSERIE to PLœches and relieved the 1st WILTS. Heavy firing on our left all night at Hill 60. Casualties	

WAR DIARY or INTELLIGENCE SUMMARY.

(Erase heading not required.)

Hour, Date, Place	Summary of Events and Information	Remarks and references to Appendices
APRIL 20th Cont	During relief. Pte EF GARDINER B Coy killed - L.Cpl DT JONES C.Coy, Pte RN MERRY C.Coy and SH BEDFORD D Coy wounded.	
21st ST ELOI	In Trenches. Quiet in our sector. Few whizz bangs in morning. Shell heard a great deal of firing at Hill 60. Germans start shelling YPRES with 17" howitzer - heard that we shell Hill 60. Casualties nil. Fine day.	
22nd ST ELOI	Quiet morning in trenches. Shell fighting at Hill 60. YPRES heavily shelled. Heavy firing during night N. of YPRES. The CO. visited O.C.'s all trenches of likelihood of an attack. Casualties Pte M. GREEN A Coy killed. Cpl AF VERTUE B Coy died of wounds in LA CLYTTE hospital and buried in Cemetry there L.Cpl CM. DRON C. Coy and Cpl N.T. ASTLEY D. Coy wounded. Pte RS MILLER A. Coy Cpl CO. HENFREY C. Coy, L.Cpl C. EB HAYNES A.Coy wounded.	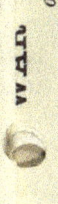
23rd ST ELOI	Heavy firing all day North of YPRES. Quiet day in trenches. [Seaj Major R. GREEN of C Coy killed in P2.	

INTELLIGENCE SUMMARY

Army Form C. 2118.

WAR DIARY or INTELLIGENCE SUMMARY.
(Erase heading not required.)

Instructions regarding War Diaries and Intelligence Summaries are contained in F.S. Regs., Part II. and the Staff Manual respectively. Title pages will be prepared in manuscript.

Hour, Date, Place	Summary of Events and Information	Remarks and references to Appendices
APRIL. 23rd (contd) ST ELOI	German aeroplanes active in Evening Signalling. Other casualties. Cpl J T MADELEY A Coy. Pte L F HORNE T CORNER, and R L VINER wounded.	
24th	German shelling all day. Started early shelling the wood round S.P. and in the afternoon P 4.6 had a Shell in Killing 1 and wounding 5 of A Coy. Relieved by the WILTSHIRE Regt in the Evening at about 9.30 - 10. and returned to DICKEBUSCH. Casualties. Casualties B Coy J.G. GRAHAME A Coy killed. Pte CA SPEYER, GJ MANSFIELD, CJ HUNT, D Coy, LF COOKE, JO ABBOTT + A HOARE A Stewart C Coy. L. Cpl PC RICHARDS, EE DAVIES, AV STEWART, AAB BROOKE, HM PHILLIPS and Sgt HS DIX all A Coy wounded. A severe casualty list fr 4 days of 2 Killed and wounded. We has that the MILTS had been standing to into our packed up for last two days. Fine day tpt by wet night.	
25th DICKEBUSCH	In billets. Carrying fatigue of 50 from Each Company.	

Hour, Date, Place	Summary of Events and Information	Remarks and references to Appendices
APRIL 25th DICKEBUSCH (cont.)	with Mr BLAKE, Mr ASCOUGH, Mr HOARE and Mr NOBLE carrying material to the trenches in the evening. We hear that Hill 60 is now absolutely in our hands. The day. Heard that the draft will be up to-morrow.	
26th DICKEBUSCH	In billets. 12 N.C.O.s + men from A + C. Coys grenade throwing in the morning behind R.E. Park. Were shelled in the evening by shrapnel and had several casualties. Fatigue parties go from each company carrying material to the trenches. Casualties P&Ly BENHAM A.Coy killed. Sergt F.T.GALLOWAY, Cpl SPRIGDEN. HS STEPHENS. Pte JAB PAUL, L.H.SHELLEY, A.C.NEAL, C.S.KERIN, DY HARRIS. WS COOK, F.COHEN, A.Coy, H.B. HOBLYN C.Coy J.T. BUDIBENT, P RODD + E.B. DODWELL D.Coy.	
27th DICKEBUSCH	The General Officer Commanding 7th Brigade inspected Bn Hq Grenadiers in morning. Shelled from two sides in middle day. Shrapnel from the front pacroom from 1/2 left rear in evening. Several casualties in the village - ours a few only. Fatigue parties go from each company in evening. Dickebusch becoming very unhealthy. L.G. HARRIS D Coy wounded.	

WAR DIARY
INTELLIGENCE SUMMARY.
(Erase heading not required.)

Army Form C. 2118.

Hour, Date, Place	Summary of Events and Information	Remarks and references to Appendices
APRIL 28th DICKEBUSCH	A + D Coys left Billets at 5 AM + went back about a mile to back of DICKEBUSCH to woods + hedges for day. C.O. + Captains of Coys met to settle distribution of Coys in trenches. A in reserve for first two days. C in P2 + P3. B. P7A, P4B, P6. P5 new. D in P2A, P4 + P5. Left DICKEBUSCH at 7.30 + moved to P trenches to relieve the WILTS. REGT. Relief completed without casualty. Fine day.	
29th ST ELOI.	In trenches. Quiet day. Redoubt shelled by whizz-bangs - not much damage done. Reserve Coy building huts + shelters in wood near Headquarter farm.	
30th ST ELOI	In trenches quiet day. A Coy relieved C Coy in P2 + P3. Fine day.	

(signed) W. J. Woodgate

7th Inf.Bde.
3rd Div.

WAR DIARY

1st BATTN. THE HONOURABLE ARTILLERY COMPANY.

M A Y

1 9 1 5

WAR DIARY
or
INTELLIGENCE SUMMARY.

Army Form C. 2118.

Hour, Date, Place	Summary of Events and Information	Remarks and references to Appendices
MAY.		
1st ST ELOI	In trenches. Quiet day. Fine weather.	
2nd ST ELOI.	Cas<sup>ties</sup> MAY 2nd: Pte OSSTEMBRIDGE (A) col killed. A.L. SKINNER (B) C.E. SONRY (A) wounded. In trenches. Heavy enemy artillery during after noon to North. German guns slightly shelled all trenches + shrapnel over the back. About 8.30 sudden outburst of firing to NORTH (vicinity of Hill 60) all quiet in B hour. WILTS REGT relieved us at about 9.30-10. P.m. Same. C.O. and Batt<sup>n</sup> returned to DICKEBUSCH. [killed struck in same. C.O. and all trenches have map into heavy during the afternoon. (Casualties. Pte H.G.BARNES C. Coy R.S.CASLON + R.G.JONES B Coy wounded, date MAY 1st)	
3rd DICKEBUSCH.	In Billets. Few shells over in early morning. Fatigue party in evening under Captain HOLLIDAY 50 from each company.	
	Casualties. Pte F.E. CLARKE (wd MAY 2) died of wounds. Saf<sup>ty</sup> R.E. HOARE + Mr BAZIN dying on communication trench Mr SCHIFF, Mr DAVIS, Mr JORGENSEN (C), Pte B.T. HOWSE (B) + F.T. NICHOLLS (A) wounded.	

WAR DIARY
or
INTELLIGENCE SUMMARY.
(Erase heading not required.)

Army Form C. 2118.

Hour, Date, Place	Summary of Events and Information	Remarks and references to Appendices
MAY		
4th DICKEBUSCH.	In billets.	
5th DICKEBUSCH	In billets	
6th DICKEBUSCH	In billets - The Germans started shelling the village in morning. A Coy moved to Transport Field. In evening all companies except B. moved to Huts in RIDGEWOOD and took over from R.I.R. and 4th SOUTH LANCS. Head quarters remained in DICKEBUSCH. B. coy remained in farm S.E of PIONEER FARM. Fine weather.	
7th RIDGEWOOD	Working on dug outs in trench line at back of wood. Fatigues in evening. 60 of each Company carrying A & D. under Mr MURPHY & Mr ELLIS to J	

WAR DIARY or INTELLIGENCE SUMMARY.

Army Form C. 2118.

Hour, Date, Place	Summary of Events and Information	Remarks and references to Appendices
7th RIDGEWOOD	B + C. with Mr BRONTON, MR MCARTHUR to S.8. Casualties. Nil.	
8th RIDGEWOOD	Working on Dug outs &c. In evening 100 A Coy with Mr REED, 100 B Coy with Mr STURT. carrying material re. to S.8. Continues fine weather. Casualties. Pte M H COTTON + P&G E PORTER D Coy wounded.	
9th RIDGEWOOD	Working on Dug outs &c. Fatigue parties in evening. 50 A Coy with Mr SCHIFF. carrying. C Coy digging trenches between P.2 + P.5. YPRES in flames. Casualties. Cpl L R HUMPHRYS Pte A H J DANIELS + P&G F DAVIES A Coy wounded (the latter since of wounds on MAY 10th) Shell in dug outs. Fatigue of practically the whole Battalion carrying up material re. in the evening. YPRES shell burning. Fine weather.	

INTELLIGENCE SUMMARY

WAR DIARY
or
INTELLIGENCE SUMMARY.

Army Form C. 2118.

Hour, Date, Place	Summary of Events and Information	Remarks and references to Appendices
11a RIDGEWOOD	Still in my wts rc.	
12a.	LfftRIDGEWOOD in the evening to the relieve the WILTS REGT in the P trenches	

INTELLIGENCE SUMMARY.

(Erase heading not required.)

Army Form C. 2118.

Hour, Date, Place	Summary of Events and Information	Remarks and references to Appendices
11th RIDGEWOOD	Headquarters now at PIONEER FARM. Left the wood in evening to relieve 1st WILTS REGT in the trenches. A Coy P2 & P3. B coy P2A, P4, P4A. C coy P5 & 6. D coy in reserve. YPRES shell burning CAPT GARNSEY & LIEUT BLAKE went down unwell.	
12th ELZENWALLE	In trenches. Quiet day. [Casualties. Pte F.W. BARNES. A coy, killed. Pte A.G. RHODES. A coy wounded by shell in trenches at WILTS HOUSE.	
13th ELZENWALLE	In trenches. Quiet day. Shell burst at WILTS HOUSE. Attack on right at 6.30 in evening of party in F5 or G5, lost, then stood to. Changed over in evening. A to P5 + 6. B to reserve. C to P1, P2 & P3. D to P2A, P4. Pte A.B. Casualties L/Cpl. C.R. EAST. A coy killed.	
14th ELZENWALLE	In trenches. Quiet day. L/Cpl. W.M. PHILLIPS. A coy killed.	

INTELLIGENCE SUMMARY.

(Erase heading not required.)

Hour, Date, Place	Summary of Events and Information	Remarks and references to Appendices
MAY		
15. ELZENWALLE	In trenches. Redoubt S.P. completed by the R.A.E. and South Lancs Pioneers and taken over by the WILTS. REGT. Head Quarters moved to the BRASSERIE. ELZENWALLE. Casualties. Pte F.H.B. FAWLEY. A Coy killed. Pte H.W.BROWN (C) Pte F.STOTT (D) + Pte F.T.WAKEFIELD.(B) wounded.	
16. ELZENWALLE.	In trenches. Quiet day. Some change in trenches in evening. Casualties. Pte R.V. HEDDERWICK D Coy killed. Pte S.BARTLETT. D Coy wounded.	
17. ELZENWALLE.	In trenches. Zeppelin sighted in N. direction at 3.30 AM. apparently disabled. Heard heavy firing in South all day. Relieved by the WILTS REGT in evening. a very dark night. Germans opened fire on our left by the farm - ans in front delayed relief. Reliefs had great difficulty owing to darkness and wet condition of ground. Wet day.	

WAR DIARY
or
INTELLIGENCE SUMMARY.
(Erase heading not required.)

Army Form C. 2118.

Hour, Date, Place	Summary of Events and Information	Remarks and references to Appendices
MAY.		
18th RIDGEWOOD &c.	A. Coy went to Farm near PIONEER FARM. C & Farm further S.W. B & D in RIDGEWOOD. Casualties - Sergt S MUNT, Pte A. R. SIEN (S) B Coy wounded. In billets. H.Q. in Pioneer Farm. Dull river.	
19th RIDGEWOOD &c.	In billets. Fatigue party 40 C. Coy in evening carrying huts & trestles to BRASSERIE. Dull.	
20th RIDGEWOOD &c.	In billets. Fine day.	
21st RIDGEWOOD &c.	In billets. Relieved the WILTS REGT. in Phéuchio A Coy in trenches at BRASSERIE. B Coy P1, 2, 23. C Coy in P5 + 6. D in P2A. P4, A+B. Relief completed without loss. H.Q. at BRASSERIE. Fatigue party A Coy in small parties carrying mg.	

Army Form C. 2118.

INTELLIGENCE SUMMARY.

(Erase heading not required.)

Instructions regarding War Diaries and Intelligence Summaries are contained in F.S. Regs., Part II. and the Staff Manual respectively. Title pages will be prepared in manuscript.

Hour, Date, Place	Summary of Events and Information	Remarks and references to Appendices
MAY. 21st (cont.)	Sandbags &c to R trenches. Fine day. PteG ROSE Signaller wounded.	
22nd ELZENWALLE	In trenches. Fine day — Thunder storm in evening. Fatigue parties & coy carrying sandbags, duckwalks &c to trenches at night.	
23rd ELZENWALLE	In trenches. Aeroplanes very active in morning.	
24" ditto	In trenches. During day a shell from one of our own batteries through driving round very defective burst over the RIDGEWOOD where the Colonel & Brigade Major were walking and burst in a field just in front of our dressing station. M. Mess. any Worthy & Newton	

Forms/C. 2118/10

INTELLIGENCE SUMMARY.

(Erase heading not required.)

Army Form C. 2118.

Hour, Date, Place	Summary of Events and Information	Remarks and references to Appendices
	was slung up & taken to Brigade H.Q. — In the evening about 5 p.m. all trenches reported the men were suffering with soreness irritation of the eyes — it was also noticed by adjutant on way up from DICKEBUSCH. By some it was attributed to some powder having been dropped by enemy aeroplanes. There was a peculiar sweet smell noticed in air in late evening. I therefore think was due to return times there was warmer to be extra vigilant in case it was some further attempt at fright: there my enemy & no dark rumor it was retiring by. There was of asphyxiating gas by enemy & troops on our left — in noise of bombardment	

INTELLIGENCE SUMMARY.

Army Form C. 2118.

(Erase heading not required.)

Hour, Date, Place	Summary of Events and Information	Remarks and references to Appendices

At YPRES - Many of men in trenches were reduced to mending woollies owing to their eyes being made to smart & water so much. The advices had no shields during the night - & the next day from this cause - several casualties today. Wounded only - Sergt. J.C. VERNON (C Company) Ptes. CARR H.O & ROY. P.L. (both B Company) and Pte ROBINSON W.D. (D Company) the latter by a piece of shell fusing from guns of our own anti aircraft Battys. which were very busy today. so shots at me however were corrected as I was at me of our own planes by enemy batteries and I merely saw our planes were very active and daring

WAR DIARY or INTELLIGENCE SUMMARY.

Army Form C. 2118.

(Erase heading not required.)

Instructions regarding War Diaries and Intelligence Summaries are contained in F. S. Regs., Part II. and the Staff Manual respectively. Title pages will be prepared in manuscript.

Hour, Date, Place	Summary of Events and Information	Remarks and references to Appendices
MAY.		
25th ELZENWALLE	In trenches. Quiet day & relieved at night by WILTS – went to RIDGEWOOD to rest & biling as Brigade reserve – No casualties –	
26th RIDGEWOOD	In billets – Fine weather – Dugouts	
27th ditto	ditto. Men in dugouts – No shelling	
	New fatigue parties of 100–200 men at night carrying up trench stores – some very heavy work done than as all stores carried up from ELZENWALLE	
28th ditto	Men in dugouts. Stores for engineers taken up every night – & parties very large – great heat of trenches are trying matters – The difficulty of getting hot food cooked rather in excess rock to trenches in dugouts –	

INTELLIGENCE SUMMARY.

(Erase heading not required.)

Hour, Date, Place	Summary of Events and Information	Remarks and references to Appendices
RIDGWOOD. 29th May.	In dugouts as reserve to Bde. Working & carrying parties as before.	
30 May. ELLENWALLE	BRASSERIE - Rather unpleasant on the way up. One of B Coy killed PTE BATEMAN. F.M. (C Company) Wounded Sergt MEEHAN (C.F.) (C Company) Sergt Morris A.O. & Pte TURNER G. (both of A Company) all by rifle fire. Weather fine.	
31 May. ditto	Still in P trenches. Quiet: every fine.	

1st H.A.C
War Diaries for periods
17-6-15 to 24-10-15 inc.
are missing

7th Inf.Bde.
3rd Div.

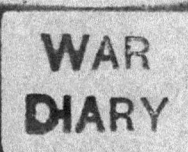

1st BATTN. THE HONOURABLE ARTILLERY COMPANY.

J U N E

(1.6.15 to 16.6.15)

1 9 1 5

WAR DIARY or INTELLIGENCE SUMMARY

Army Form C. 2118.

III. 1 H A C

Hour, Date, Place	Summary of Events and Information	Remarks and references to Appendices
1915		VC 1. 4. 5. 6. 7. 8 9. 10. 11. & 12
1 June ELZENWALLE	In P Trenches. Relief of trenches by companys at night. Very quiet day. A Company relieved D Coy in front line. Wounded Pte RUSSELL Nº P. Coy)	
2 June do	In P Trenches. Quiet day. Killed. Sergt. Baker Browne A. Coy. who had been recommended for a commission in Regt. was struck on lunge in early morning & died received Pte relief tonight by Pte WELFORD. A-H. (C Company) Orders received for relief tonight by 85th Rifle and we are leaving area — Wounded (Lt. WILLINGALE (B Coy) W. J. We left P trenches & marched to bivouac field near VLAMERTINGHE arriving in are going into	
VLAMERTINGHE 3 June do	Arrived & bivouacked in field near here. Every body very weary after a trying	

WAR DIARY
or
INTELLIGENCE SUMMARY.

(Erase heading not required.)

Army Form C. 2118.

Hour, Date, Place	Summary of Events and Information	Remarks and references to Appendices
3 Jun 1915. VLAMERTINGHE	night spent in a very long which followed by a long march. Every indication of a complete change of scene - fine + warm	
4 Jun ditto	visit in morning on field Hospital Inspection which is to be into YPRES before going in into trenches which are in HOOGE district. Everyone rather introduced at the change. Received word we are to relieve the Dragoon Guards that - an unknown amount of work is needed in trenches. fine. 2 officers went to the RAMPARTS - YPRES today to view the dugouts to be occupied	
5 Jun ditto	Battalion has orders to go to RAMPARTS YPRES today & spent morn my report mg. & were then inspected by C.O. In af ter- noon Battalion marched off via VLAMERTINGHE.	

WAR DIARY or INTELLIGENCE SUMMARY

Army Form C. 2118.

Hour, Date, Place	Summary of Events and Information	Remarks and references to Appendices
5 June. YPRES.	Arrived at about 7 p.m. and relieved 3rd Dragoon Guards of Cavalry Division in HOOGE Street. The recruits dug into during in YPRES soon after arriving were men were getting into billets the Ramparts were breeched a usual occurrence in the afternoon – several shells fell near the billets & one into room in which the Machine Gunners were – Pte PILGRIM.P. (B Sqn) Killed & wounded Pte LEMMON.M.H. (since 8/6/15) (B L.M) Pte HAME A.W. (C Sqn) & Cpl. CHARLES L.P. First 3 names were civilian names & the firm casualties among this section. The rest of the company in escaped quite free. The dugouts were not too good except those attached in the walls of the Ramparts	

WAR DIARY or INTELLIGENCE SUMMARY

Army Form C. 2118.

Hour, Date, Place	Summary of Events and Information	Remarks and references to Appendices
6th June YPRES.	All companies & H.Q. in Ramparts. Work being cleaning up during day & heavy fatigue parties during night. The town in a terrible state of destruction though fairly clean as far as trenches go owing to work done by engineers cleaning parties. A great deal has been burnt down by them and in places burning is still going on. Early in morning a pigeon alighting on a wet trench-down a large tile on the head of & wounded Pte Fairhead (boy). Some shelling of the town about the square by shrapnel. At night the whole of the available men (over 400) went up to HOOGE carrying bombs & very heavy & long fatigue. Most of rest & very ready & long fatigue marched were knife the men had bruised shoulders next day.	

Hour, Date, Place	Summary of Events and Information	Remarks and references to Appendices
6 June YPRES	and the procession on night fire must have worried for a man & with. Capt. DOUGLAS was in charge & with only 2 guides great difficulty was experienced in keeping men closed up about HOOGE The place was very lively and 3 men were hit during the journey. Lieut G. SCOTT-ROBERTSON (C Coy) HUNT. H.F. (D Coy) & KRAUSS. N.D. (C Coy) The fatigue party were all just clear back from Firing line as enemy fire came & on by running on a heavy burst of rifle fire made things lively near Pte D. CLARE was however lifted off his feet by a ricochet bullet on heel of his boot.	
7 June YPRES	Were in RAMPARTS turning up and fatigue parties. Major WARD and O.C.'s Coys went up to HOOGE to go over	

WAR DIARY or INTELLIGENCE SUMMARY

Army Form C. 2118.

(Erase heading not required.)

Hour, Date, Place	Summary of Events and Information	Remarks and references to Appendices
7 June YPRES.	Trenches at HOOGE where we are re-relieving the WILTS tomorrow night. The party was sniped at while going over the open country from HILL 60.	
8 June YPRES.	In Ramparts morning day, and preparing for relief of WILTS tonight. Left at 8 p.m. by the Menin Gate Bridge. D Coy leading, and some shrapnel was met but no dummy now - near HOOGE. Whole line was very hot - 2 men of D Coy had equipment hit. D Coy is in right sector opposite CHATEAU & the WALL (H 13 & 14 inners) & B Coy in left sector & the STABLE & support (H15 16 17). A & C Coys (& H.Q.) being in ZOUAVE in support. No casualties during relief.	

WAR DIARY
or
INTELLIGENCE SUMMARY.
(Erase heading not required.)

Army Form C. 2118.

Hour, Date, Place	Summary of Events and Information	Remarks and references to Appendices
9 June. HOOGE.	Fairly quiet day — most notable thing that in this sector thing practically the apex of the Salient rifle fire is from all sides & the rear even. Snipers not at all great having now practically non-existent trenches the 3 Divns can have. The enemy very rarely ever showing himself and great deal — evidently averse to expose anything & no target yet. Have targets for our men I have today their own sniper. Much work in improving parapets. In no places of right sector enemy just other side of a barricade across in the trench of own — and our men can hear rumour & talking quite plainly. This is a bombing post near STABLE. General not during day in stable especially	

WAR DIARY or INTELLIGENCE SUMMARY

Army Form C. 2118.

Hour, Date, Place	Summary of Events and Information	Remarks and references to Appendices
9th June HOOGE	Pte. MEDHURST. E.H. Coy runner wounded in dug-out in ZOUAVE WOOD. Pte. TRIPP. C.C. WILSON. A.L. YEATMAN. A.A.R. Coy. and SWIFT. C.E. & ROBERTS. C. D Coy. all wounded. Weather fine.	
10 June HOOGE	Some shelling of left sector during day. During rifle fire day & night — a very noisy shot sniper. Much burying and our front. We have never reported them so much appalling offences as now, men even hit in SILVER men which is very infrequent. My CHATEAU wounded today. Lieut. FIELD. C. FARMER.S. LAVENDER.F. BALDCHIN. J.R.A. & Capt. McQUEEN.E.F. Weather fine. C. Company relieved D Coy & A. Coy relieved B Coy. at night.	

WAR DIARY
or
INTELLIGENCE SUMMARY.
(Erase heading not required.)

Army Form C. 2118.

Hour, Date, Place	Summary of Events and Information	Remarks and references to Appendices
11. June. HOOGE.	Enemy very quiet after prior enemy getting more & more annoying and troublesome - mining started at 5.30 in direction of CHATEAU. Also some tunnelling mine - Heavy fatigues parties for Miners purpose at night. Wounded Ptes ROGERS.P.G. CUTLER.G. HAYNES.A.C. KING.E.J. & HILL.C.L.G. Relieved by another Division this night moving up 12? further wounded. CORPL MORPHY.K. Pte HULL.WM. Sergt TODD.H.G. & 2/8 pm BEVINGTON.R.J. Enemy work on transport field at "---" for use: spent day cleaning	
12. June.	up & refitting.	
13. June.	Still in rest billets. Rumours of our Divison being about to attack at HOOGE. C.O. has conference and	

Army Form C. 2118.

WAR DIARY
or
INTELLIGENCE SUMMARY.
(Erase heading not required.)

Hour, Date, Place	Summary of Events and Information	Remarks and references to Appendices
14 June.	instructions in any and should us Brew H.Q. in afternoon. Definite orders received of attack on Y. WOOD. By 3rd Division on 16th inst. and that we share in attack in support with us- of 7th Bde. and being notified and rifles & equipment issued during day. In afternoon L.O. had a conference with Officers and gave detailed views as to disposition of battalion in attack, as follows:- One Battalion being in position in assembly trenches nearly any behind support line Nth with Y. WOOD with 2 companies from right to left being D.B.C.A.	

WAR DIARY
or
INTELLIGENCE SUMMARY.
(Erase heading not required.)

Army Form C. 2118.

Hour, Date, Place	Summary of Events and Information	Remarks and references to Appendices

when the front attacking line which consisted of units of 9th Batt. reached the first German line the H.A.C. were to move forward + occupy + consolidate the position won. D Company to take the right of this position + establish connection with WILTS who would attack position from right of Ward to MENIN ROAD B Company to occupy centre and C Coy to take left. Flank 2 platoons of A Coy to move up also + my communication trench back to our original line was remainder of A Coy to start same trench from that line forward to German line. Spades picks &c carried by A Coy. and every man 2 flings of S.A.A. extra. Major Ward + 2 men for each company were detailed to go up to time of

WAR DIARY
or
INTELLIGENCE SUMMARY.
(Erase heading not required.)

Army Form C. 2118.

Hour, Date, Place	Summary of Events and Information	Remarks and references to Appendices
15 June	country. Viewed tonight reconnoitre roads as country. Remainder of afternoon was spent in explaining plan roles to men & N.C.O's. Every one very bright at prospect of having a blow at the Huns we have been watching so long & there were some sing-songs in the evening. Busy morning getting ready to move. Left HAYDEN party in reserve at B & coy and Mr TATHAM reserve 2/Lt commanding D Coomby. Some discussion during morning as to plans. Battalion paraded at 2 p.m. and C.O. gave a few words about the good work the regiment already and being upheld and then battalion marched to KRUISSTRADT where plan of advancing of 3 Inn was and to halt & move on as the spot was	

WAR DIARY or INTELLIGENCE SUMMARY.

Army Form C. 2118.

Hour, Date, Place	Summary of Events and Information	Remarks and references to Appendices

June 16 1915 —

reached our emplaning [entraining] area marching via seven fields. A Hun airplane was being shelled above by our guns and a small shell dropped into the centre of the field just missing tail of D Coy, but not exploding. On reaching ZONNEBEKE a wounded Capt. WALSH the Adjutant in the rear and in next to it taken away in ambulance Capt. OSMOND was appointed Adj/Regt. Major WARD who arrived here reported their company Pioneers had been heavily shelled already. Left were of assembly at 9 p.m. marched via MENIN. YPRES Railway and MENIN Road to the assembly trenches in front of Y WOOD which were reached without casualty — and about

2 A.M. some difficulty experienced in getting

WAR DIARY
or
INTELLIGENCE SUMMARY.
(Erase heading not required.)

Army Form C. 2118.

Hour, Date, Place	Summary of Events and Information	Remarks and references to Appendices
	Took over the at WITTEPORT FARM having been badly shelled. All coys in their positions with H.Q. in dug outs just in support. Line was very heavily shelled by our own artillery when enemy trenches began to be heavily shelled by enemy guns. When our bombardment was timed to begin at dawn our guns opened and terrific shelling of Y WOOD began. Enemy replied vigorously & promptly & support line was very warmly shelled. Nothing could be seen owing to clouds of smoke of the German lines & attacking parties were lost to sight. H.A.C. & Munster LINCOLNS & Royal Irish support line & thence into front line trenches in advance when attack pushed forward — Colonel & Major WARD were hit early in morning as the Battalion was advancing from	

WAR DIARY
or
INTELLIGENCE SUMMARY.
(Erase heading not required.)

Army Form C. 2118.

Hour, Date, Place	Summary of Events and Information	Remarks and references to Appendices
	from the British firing line and also telephonic communication had been opened up which I beg was over Battn H.Q. Capt. DOUGLAS was relieved by the Colonel to take charge of the Battn. I claimed report as interior to G.O.C.) Roll is appended. Capt LANKESTER was hit whilst digging the C.T. together BOYLE also during consolidation of 1st German line trench position. Mr. HOARE was mortally wounded in the enemy's trench as soon as he arrived there. Mr TATHAM was also mortally wounded 5th april. There being several machine guns turned on the right of the WOOD position by Germans line from positions in BELLEWARDE FARM. Attack was with pressed forward into the 3rd German line but our own troops experienced much shelling from our own artillery	

WAR DIARY
or
INTELLIGENCE SUMMARY.
(Erase heading not required.)

Army Form C. 2118.

Instructions regarding War Diaries and Intelligence Summaries are contained in F. S. Regs., Part II. and the Staff Manual respectively. Title pages will be prepared in manuscript.

Hour, Date, Place	Summary of Events and Information	Remarks and references to Appendices
	and were unable to advance so much as required on the right & the Wilts being unable to reach out of the River which they had reached our right was exposed & continuation of the line in that direction urgent. During the morning very heavy shelling of this line developed and many casualties occurred & D Company moved further forward to form a communication trench in from of I wood as right front. Trenches under circs. are B Company remain in the original German line but on left the attack having got further down are there parts of C & 6 of A & B got into advanced positions	

WAR DIARY or INTELLIGENCE SUMMARY

Army Form C. 2118.

Hour, Date, Place	Summary of Events and Information	Remarks and references to Appendices
	C Company were ordered forward by Lieut Colonel J. T. Rose to re-inforce that attack which had penetrated as far as 3rd German line but was going on way to German line. Party of C Company 2/Lt McARTHUR & 11 Platoon of C Company went forward & later was reinforced by Portion of A Company but were unable to hold when forward portions later when by fire when ranked officers there. Owing though stopped by our own artillery army to very heavy enemy shelling which was then & falling back & troops on left of C to A Company the 2nd German line could no no longer seen & their parties fell back on rear of their companies in the original German line.	

WAR DIARY
or
INTELLIGENCE SUMMARY.
(Erase heading not required.)

Army Form C. 2118.

Instructions regarding War Diaries and Intelligence Summaries are contained in F. S. Regs., Part II. and the Staff Manual respectively. Title pages will be prepared in manuscript.

Place	Date	Hour	Summary of Events and Information	Remarks and references to Appendices
			... all companies of H.A.C. were during rest of day until relieved accept D Company which was occupying communication trench forward of WOOD with LINCOLNS in front and WILTS on the right.	

www.ingramcontent.com/pod-product-compliance
Lightning Source LLC
Chambersburg PA
CBHW081433160426
43193CB00013B/2269